TRANSITION

Resources For and Stories About Veterans Transitioning to Civilian Life

Peter J. Burke, EdD.

TRANSITION: Resources For and Stories About Veterans Transitioning to Civilian Life; Copyright © 2025 by Dr. Peter J. Burke, EdD.

All rights reserved. No parts of this publication may be reproduced, distributed, or transmitted in any form or by any means, including photocopying, recording, or other electronic or mechanical methods, without the prior written permission of the publisher, except in cases of brief quotations embodied in critical reviews and certain other noncommercial uses permitted by copyright law.

Prominence Publishing
www.prominencepublishing.com

Content review and editorial comments provided by Rita M. Reali, the Persnickety Proofreader, and by Jennifer Parrish, M.Ed., LBA, BCBA

Editing by Burke R & W Services

Transition: Resources For and Stories About Veterans Transitioning to Civilian Life/Dr. Peter J. Burke, EdD. - 1st edition

ISBN: 978-1-997649-08-3

Table of Contents

List of VA and Important Numbers 1

Thanks and Dedication 3

About the Author 5

Chapter 1: Military Culture vs. Civilian Culture 7

    Structure vs. Flexibility 9

    Deployments and Traveling 11

    Military Culture vs. Societal Expectations and Standards 15

Chapter 2: My Story 23

    The Beginning of the End 23

    Out-Processing 24

    Family 27

    Financial 29

    Substance Use 29

    Homelessness 33

    Mental Health 35

    Legal Matters 38

    Exit Services Upon ETS/Retirement (then) 40

Chapter 3: Other Obstacles to Transitioning 41

Sources.. 41

Employment 43

Finances.. 44

Neurological Concerns.. 45

Suicide Risk 46

Stigmas 48

Lack of "Reciprocal" Credentials........................... 52

Skills Translation- Resume vs. Skills List, Translation.. 53

Job/Career/Unemployment................................. 54

Education 55

Academic Support... 58

Chapter 4: Available Resources to Facilitate Transitioning... 61

Department of Defense (DoD)/Service Branches... 64

DoD- Transition Assistance Program (TAP)........ 65

U.S. Department of Veterans Affairs (VA) 66

VA- Transition Programs 67

VA- Health 68

VA- Mental Health 72

VA- Support and Family Education (SAFE)
    Program 74
VA- Veterans Integration to Academic Life
    (VITAL) Initiative.. 74
VA- Homeless Patient Aligned Care Team
    (HPACT) Model.. 78
VA- Education and Training................................ 79
VA- Veteran Readiness & Employment (VR&E). 84
Civilian Organizations 85
Veterans Service Organization (VSO) 86
Student Veterans of America (SVA) 86
SVA- MySVA Portal 87
SVA- My Success Hub 87
SVA- APEX 91
SVA- Programs 92
SVA- Advocacy 94
SVA- Community Service 96
American Legion (Legion).................................... 97
Legion- Advocacy... 98
Legion- Community Service................................. 99
Veterans of Foreign Wars (VFW)........................ 100
VFW- Advocacy... 101
VFW- Community Service.................................. 102
VFW- Programs... 102

Wounded Warrior Project (WWP) 103
WWP- Advocacy 104
WWP- Community Service 104
Disabled American Veterans (DAV) 105
DAV- Advocacy 106
DAV- Community Service 107
Iraq & Afghanistan Veterans of America
    (IAVA) 108
IAVA- Advocacy 108
Paralyzed Veterans of America (PVA) 110
PVA- Advocacy 110
PVA- Community Service 111
Academic Organizations 112
Academic- Veteran Service Organizations/
    Veteran Student Organizations on Campus .. 113
Non-Academic 114
Hire Heroes USA 114
Fisher House Foundation 115
Elizabeth Dole Foundation (EDF) 117
National Veterans Foundation (NVF) 119
United Service Organization (USO) 121
Tragedy Assistance Program for Veterans
    Survivors (TAPS) 126
Operation Home Front 129

    Vet Dogs 131

    Warriors in Need (WIN) 134

    PTSD Foundation of America/Camp Hope 135

    Camp Hope 137

    Operation Song... 140

    Family, Friends, and Normalcy 141

    Peer-to-Peer Suggested Methodologies 144

    Social Media 148

    Team Rubicon 149

    Institute for Veterans & Military Families
       (IVMF) 149

Chapter 5: The Journey 151

    The "Feeling" 155

Chapter 6: Other Veterans' Experiences—
   Your Story Matters!.. 159

    Caitlyn Van Dam.. 159

    Omar Reynoso 164

    Ralph Figueroa... 170

    Shena R. Veale 175

References 181

List of VA and Important Numbers

Veterans Crisis Line ....Dial 988, then Press 1

VA Hotline... 800-MYVA411
(800-698-2411, option 9)

MyVA411..800-698-2411

Bereavement Counseling
(through Vet Centers) 877-927-8387

Camp Lejeune Family Member
Program 866-372-1144

Civilian Health and Medical Program
(CHAMPVA).. 800-733-8387

Community Care Billing Questions 877-881-7618

Debt Management Center 800-827-0648

Education 888-442-4551

Foreign Medical Program 877-345-8179
or 303-331-7590

Headstones and Markers 800-697-6947

Health Care 877-222-8387

Homeless Veterans 877-424-3838

Home Loans 877-827-3702

Life Insurance, All Programs other than
SGLI, FSGLI, TSGLI, VGLI 800-669-8477

Life Insurance, Veterans' Group Life Insurance
Program (VGLI), Claims for Service Members'
Group Life Insurance (SGLI) and
Family SGLI 800-419-1473

National Cemetery Scheduling Office 800-535-1117

Native American Direct Home Loans.......888-349-7541

Presidential Memorial Certificate
Program 202-565-4964

Spina Bifida Program 888-820-1756

TTY, Federal Relay 711

VA Benefits...800-827-1000

Vet Center Call Center............................877-927-8387

Women Veterans...877-222-8387

72-Hour Emergency Care Notification
Line 844-724-7842

Thanks and Dedication

I would like to thank Rita M. Reali, my cousin and Persnickety Proofreader, for reviewing my manuscript and providing valuable comments and editing advice. I hadn't realized that I said "that" so often; I write like I (and the rest of my family) talk in our own language. I forgot the rule, if it makes sense without the word "that," then it is unnecessary. I must have said it needlessly about a thousand times, lol. Thanks for assisting with the clean-up!

I would like to thank Jennifer Parrish, M.Ed., LBA, BCBA, for her review and assistance with clarifications, the addition of background information, and the connection of story material through notes and additional material suggestions, which helped create a more comprehensive picture.

I want to thank Caitlyn Van Dam, SGT, U.S.M.C., for presenting their story from the heart; Omar Reynoso, SFC, U.S. Army, Retired, for providing a unique presentation that surely captures your interest; Ralph Figueroa, CPL, U.S. Army, for his longitudinal presentation of life as it is as a student-veteran; and Shena R. Veale, SSG, U.S. Army, for her presentation of the military life both in the National Guard and on active duty, and the importance of preparing for the transition to civilian life. These stories show various perspectives on the transition process, both triumphs and tribulations. I hope they inspire you!

This book is dedicated to Rain. She was with me for eight of her 16 years. Rain came to me as a rescue, with her older sister, Dobbie. She has comforted me in my darkest times and has helped me celebrate my successes. She would sleep next to me, by my side, every night. Rain always welcomed me home with her purr and loving meow. She played with her pack and her toys. She "sunned" herself on my bed or my desk in my office. Rain gave me unconditional love. She is a joy to have in my life. She remains with me, in my heart and memories.

About the Author

Peter J. Burke of Clarksville, Tennessee, is a researcher, author, educator, and veteran advocate. He has been a member of Kappa Kappa Psi since 1997, a member of ASCAP since 2011, affiliated with Student Veterans of America since 2021, and a member of the American Legion since 2024. Additionally, he is a Life Member of Kappa Kappa Psi. He is the Primary Investigator and Senior Writer at Burke R & W Services

Dr. Burke is a freelance researcher and a published author. His published works include *Perceptions of Student-Veterans with PTSD and Availability of Support Services in Academic Life: A Qualitative Descriptive Analysis* and *Discovering Listed PTSD Support on Campus in Higher Education: A Web Survey of Traditional Academic Institutions' Home Pages*.

His book series, A Student-Veteran's Experience with Higher Education, is an international bestseller!

A Student-Veteran's Experience with Higher Education: An Academic Journey

A Student-Veteran's Experience with Higher Education: Social, Family, and Fraternal Support…and Peppi, too!

A Student-Veteran's Experience with Higher Education: The Musical Support

Peter J. Burke, https://orcid.org/0000-0002-9118-7565

Dr. Burke resides in Tennessee with his five cats. He enjoys composing and conducting music, reading, gardening, and watching the New England Patriots.

Chapter 1

Military Culture vs. Civilian Culture

Life in the military has been well documented in film and literature. Movies such as The Green Berets, Apocalypse Now, Platoon, Saving Private Ryan, and Black Hawk Down give a serious look at military life, while movies such as Kelly's Heroes, Stripes, and You're in the Army Now (see if you can see me!) give a more comedic look at military life. Books such as Robin Moore's Green Berets, Around the World Submerged: The Voyage of the Triton, by Captain Edward L. Beach, U.S. Navy, Vietnam Uncensored: 365 Days in a Nightmare, by Jerry Glazer, U.S. Army, and A Patriot's Promise, by Israel "DT" Del Toro, Jr., U.S. Air Force, Retired, Senior Master Sergeant, provide unique views to military life underwater and on land, and their story and experiences of transition to the civilian world.

In surveys conducted by Bond et al. (2020), over 60% of post-9/11 veterans reported difficulty transitioning to civilian life, compared to 25% of veterans from earlier eras. To understand this difficulty, let us first discuss some differences between the two worlds.

Compared to the structured military lifestyle, the lack of civilian structure created challenges for veterans in organizing their lives, leading to frustration and relationship issues when interacting with people at home (Ahern et al., 2015). I retired in 1996 and got a divorce shortly afterwards. For a year, I was lost. For that time, I had lost my purpose. An incredulous incident involving a 9mm handgun in the summer of 1997 facilitated my decision to go to school. I would begin to find some structure as a student-veteran.

When I retired in 1996, I didn't know how to maintain a familiar schedule while trying to find civilian employment and stay alive and out of jail. I felt lost because I had experienced significant changes in my relationship status and my employment status. Eventually, I figured out how to deal with household activities. I didn't know how to apply for my VA benefits or where to submit my application. It wouldn't be until 2012 that I would be able to get into a Department of Veterans Affairs (VA) facility.

The lack of structure upon separation from the service often led to veterans' sense of loss of purpose, as they felt they were no longer making a notable or worthwhile contribution to a social or community effort, a common goal that involved all involved setting aside their agendas for the good of the non-Borg collective. This experience of lacking purpose or meaning was exacerbated when these same veterans struggled to find jobs that utilized their skills and experience (Ahern et al., 2015). The veterans' search for a purpose often led to their search for a new normal, for a new mission.

Structure vs. Flexibility

The rigid military structure varies dramatically from the 'freedom' of the civilian world. Veterans often found the freedom of civilian life challenging, particularly in terms of both psychological and practical aspects (Keeling, 2018). When I was in the US Army, my yearly health appointments were scheduled. I had a chow hall where I got my meals. I did not have to shop or cook when I lived in the barracks. All my medical and housing needs were provided for me by the military. Your contract, which includes benefits and pay, incorporates these costs. It wasn't free. I was not responsible for it.

Every day was scheduled for me. I could wake up and understand what would be expected of me, and when. I was told when to be where, what to do, and what to wear. The routine was built, and then maintenance was manageable. In contrast to civilian life, the military has its specific ways of doing tasks and chores. You are expected to perform your duties to the standards you were trained in. This helps with consistency of performance and being managed by the military as one of their own.

In the civilian world, I'm responsible for everything myself. I am responsible for my health and medical needs. Scheduling VA yearly care, VA mental health care, dentistry visits, the eye clinic, and the hearing clinic was a lot to add to my plate initially. As a civilian, it wasn't as easy as a one-stop chow hall to feed myself. I had to plan and execute shopping trips and take time to cook for myself. Beyond that, I had to find a place to live. Becoming a homeowner or a renter would also add stress to my situation.

Sociologically, the differences between the military and civilian worlds may intimidate veterans. During my time in the military, risqué jokes were accepted as a part of life. In the civilian world, such humor is found to be offensive. How many people understand being asked if they are a crayon eater or what their favorite Crayola crayon flavor is? Being written up at work because of a dialect, saying shit kickers instead of boots, for example, is common. Don't attempt to educate people on nautical terms misused as slang; when I did, it didn't turn out well. I was written up for my "use of language." I was being insulted by a coworker, so I provided a brief history lesson on the term's written usage, which dates back to the organized work groups or gangs on docks or ships in the 16th century. As a "Navy brat," I was also interested in nautical history. Growing up near the Mystic Seaport gave me numerous opportunities to learn about our ocean-faring heritage. A veteran, law enforcement official, government official, or hunter will understand what "range therapy" means. Most educators do not. It's not an acceptable phrase in a public school when answering a question from a fellow teacher, especially if asked what your plans are for the weekend.

Deployments and Traveling

Travel in the military is a given; it is going to happen. Most of my travels during my time of service involved aircraft, including both fixed-wing and rotary-wing types. I was not on too many ships or submarines, but there were a few. Aside from the comfortable web seating and the roomy cargo area, flights were often cozy. Traveling in the back of an M-923 5-ton truck can accommodate 16 people comfortably, or up to 26 with minimal space. Early in my military career, I learned that having a military driver's license had benefits. Driving was always more comfortable than riding in the back. Traveling to and from traffic control points, now often called security checkpoints, traveling in a convoy delivering humanitarian aid, and providing troop transport, provided me with numerous opportunities that may not have been afforded to me as a civilian, unless I was a professional driver for hazardous materials, security forces, weapons, and various munitions.

I had a memorable flight experience in a Huey during a training exercise. There is something about flying at treetop level. Those pilots were highly skilled! I remember we'd be about a foot off the ground when we'd hop out; the skids never touched green earth, not that I could tell. We had to get out in such a hurry that I felt like I was in basic training again.

Another memorable flight was on a C-130, en route to Thailand. Geographically, we were flying over interesting territory. We were on our way to Thailand for an assignment from the State Department. Relationships between the United States and that part of the region were still developing into a friendly one after the Vietnam War. A few years beforehand, I was present for the return of four POWs who were held during that conflict. Our mission was diplomatic: to facilitate positive relations between Thailand and the United States.

I thought we were close to Vietnam, but I did not know the exact flight plan. Laos or Cambodia was also between Thailand and us. This was in the early-mid-'80s. I remember our doing some evasive maneuvers: climbs, twists and rolls, dives, more rolls, and some sways. Our fighter squadron escort left us to have some fun. Only one of the escort planes remained close to us and danced our dance. You could hear communication between the pilots over the squawk box. After what seemed like a long time, we resumed our straight and level flight path, although it was probably only about five minutes. Only a few people had air sickness from the maneuvers. We landed in Bangkok, Thailand, without further incident. For those who have participated in Cobra Gold, you're welcome!

I'll remember the sights, the sounds, and the smells of military travel. There is a familiarity with flying cargo aircraft; the smells and the sounds will always be with you. So will the food. I always had something to enjoy between C-rations, MREs, and those little bag lunches with mystery slices and dry bread. I still have a few C-rations cans I saved for posterity. I tried to save some MREs, especially from the original generation. I had some for about two or three years before I ate them. I couldn't resist. Our meals depended on our flight duration, mystery meat for shorter flights, and MREs for the longer ones.

Sleeping on a military aircraft can be challenging, depending on where you are going and what you're doing. Taking a nap with your ruck and weapon between your legs differs from traveling on a military-chartered civilian aircraft.

Traveling on a civilian aircraft was once a joy. I remember that I could take my carry-on bag and not worry about bringing fraternal memorabilia (such as a paddle) or the size of my bottle of mouthwash. I could bring a pocketknife with me (blade six inches or less), one of the military's pocket "must-haves": a pen and pad of paper, a lighter (Bic or Zippo), a pocket knife, wear your "dog tags," and your military ID card were mandatory items to be carried on you. I miss traveling during these times; it's so easy, with no unreasonable restrictions.

Now, it is more time-consuming to go through check-in security and reach the gates. Back then, I'd go to the airport, get to my gate, and check in. I'd then hit one of the bars, restaurants, or travel lounges and hang out until my flight. It was relaxed. Security was present, often very present. Security was also among the most polite airport guides around!

After the attacks of 9-11, airport security tightened up dramatically. In the mid-2020s, security checks have become an expected delay, and it is expected to take an hour or more to go through the check-in security. Items such as mouthwash, toothpaste, and other personal care products are now restricted in size (in ounces or volume) and cannot be taken on an aircraft. Items that used to be brought on an airplane (such as a pocketknife), objects considered heavy, and items that could be used as a weapon (such as awards, plaques, paddles, or other memorabilia) must be in checked baggage. If you want these items that exceed the standards for inclusion in your carry-on bag to go with you, you must get them checked in a checked bag if you don't have a checked bag, or your items won't be allowed on the aircraft. One has to take their shoes off to go through security! Why? I think airport security is not as engaging with travelers as before 9/11. The best airport guides are now often airline staff or maintenance personnel who service the terminals.

As of July 8, 2025, TSA removed the requirement to remove your shoes to go through the security checkpoint. It only took 25 years.

Military Culture vs. Societal Expectations and Standards

In a study by Keeling (2018), veterans emphasized the importance of preparing for the transition from military to civilian life. A survey found that 33.3% of pre-9/11 veterans reported difficulties adjusting to civilian life, versus the 60.5% of post-9/11 veterans. They experienced numerous challenges in finding a "civilian" identity, such as veterans struggle to talk with civilians about their military service; "civilians do not understand." Veterans prefer to speak with other veterans (McCormick et al., 2019).

McCormick et al. (2019) listed characteristics that veterans identified as part of the military culture. Consistent themes included patriotism, service to our country, or "honor, duty, country." Other characteristics that military culture deems important include discipline, honor, integrity, hard work, camaraderie, order, structure, and training.

In a study by Keeling (2018), veterans stated they often feel their military jobs and skills no longer matter. Adjusting to cultural differences, such as communication styles, alertness, work ethic, and the negative impact of military service, may cause frustration and challenges in connecting. These challenges and frustrations, along with learning how to be civilians and reestablishing their identities, cause veterans to adopt new ways of being civilians (Keeling, 2018).

The military culture instills self-reliance, often in a stoic appearance. Veterans typically believe and act accordingly, prioritizing the mission's goal over personal comfort and health, often leading to the perception that sickness is a sign of weakness. The veteran's sense of pride, honor, and belief that seeking help indicates the veteran is no longer a 'hero' (Randles & Finnegan, 2021). This may lead to a loss of identity.

Civilian society possesses distinct values, characteristics, and ways of living compared to the military (McCormick et al., 2019). In the military, most perform well because people are counting on them. In the civilian world, many often get away with what they can; this was a common theme in the transition of veterans to civilian society. Other challenges for veterans included getting along with others and divorce.

In the absence of the structure provided by the military, it may feel daunting to have numerous responsibilities that offer many choices on how to fulfill them. This "freedom of choice" and personal expression are new skills to navigate the civilian world. Such a loss of structure may also lead to new opportunities and new areas to explore; transitioning veterans often find this problematic (Shue et al., 2021).

Dolan et al. (2022) stated that veterans are known to be one of the more difficult demographics to engage with, with many struggling to seek help and maintain engagement afterward. The military way of life and culture are an ethnicity in and of themselves (Dolan et al., 2022). Veterans often report struggles with their transition to civilian life, and the culture gap plays a significant role in this struggle (McCormick et al., 2019).

Transitioning from the military way of life to civilian life is complex, and trying to fit in on a college campus is a culture shock that is often difficult to do, such as the highly structured environment of the military and going to a more open-structured environment of college, being 15 years, or so, older than the traditional undergraduate student (age 18-21) or about 35 years, or so, older than the traditional students at the University of Oklahoma (OU). I was as old as, or older than, my instructors during my years at CU and OU. There was a generation gap, a culture gap, and an experience gap. I would receive inquiring looks at football games. A student my age would not often be in the stadium's student section. The transition experience had fun times; however, I know it wasn't easy. It was difficult for me.

The ASHE Higher Education Report, 2011, lists a "Hierarchy of Needs for Student-Veterans" based upon Maslow's Hierarchy of Needs from his paper A Theory of Human Motivation, from 1943. Maslow's Hierarchy of Needs is a psychological concept that applies to everyone, not just veterans. The ASHE Report is modeled after Maslow's Hierarchy of Needs, which was first introduced in 1943 and later expanded upon in his book, Motivation and Personality, published in 1954.

The base of the hierarchy of needs for student-veterans is categorized as Basic Needs. Basic needs refer to being able to address finances and health concerns. According to Maslow, this corresponds to the psychological needs identified by the bottom tier. These needs on his hierarchy include acquiring the basics of life, such as food, clothing, and shelter.

According to ASHE (2011), the next tier of the hierarchy for veterans is peer affiliation and connectedness. This correlates to Maslow's next tier, safety. Safety needs refer to the desire for a secure and predictable environment, free from threats or danger (physical or emotional). Connecting and forming relationships with fellow veterans and associating with individuals from your background or similar is comforting. This comfort translates to safety. Veterans seek out other veterans to feel safe and as if they belong. The Veteran Service Organizations (VSOs) on campus facilitate this sense of comfort and safety.

The middle tier of student-veterans' needs is "Blending In," a socialization strategy. Being accepted into the campus culture and by the student body is vital to veterans. We need to become part of our community, especially a veteran-based community. This equates to Social/Belonging, again, per Maslow. Common interests form the base of many social relationships. For me, blending in was facilitated by my involvement in the music department, specifically the Zeta Tau chapter of Kappa Kappa Psi at Cameron University, and the Delta chapters of Kappa Kappa Psi and Tau Beta Sigma at the University of Oklahoma. I was a fixture. I was always seen around the department working, rehearsing, or performing.

The second tier from the top of the "veteran's needs" concept is based on Persistence and Achievement—integration. Actions in this category may include passing a major test or exam, receiving recognition for an achievement, or receiving a scholarship. This translates to Marlow's hierarchy as Esteem. Esteem refers to a person's feeling good about themselves or having a positive outlook and perspective. Esteem is present when the effects of PTSD are being addressed; this level is difficult to achieve when one has emotional, mental, and psychological concerns or avoids treatment.

The final tier of the student-veteran hierarchy of needs is the Fulfilled Potential. Maslow's top tier of self-actualization is where all physical, intellectual, mental, emotional, and safety needs are met. The student-veteran must experience this sense of belonging and connectedness to and with the college environment (ASHE, 2011).

Hierarchy Level	Student-Veteran Needs	Maslow's Hierarchy
Top Level	Fulfilled Potential "Civilian Self"	Self-Actualization
Penultimate Level	Persistence and Achievement—integration	Esteem
Middle Level	Blending In: Socialization Strategy	Social/Belonging
Next Level	Peer affiliation and connectedness	Safety
Base	Basic Needs: Stable finances and addressed health concerns	Physiological Needs

Chapter 2

My Story

Understanding the challenges and needs of veterans during their transition to civilian life is essential for better serving them (Shue et al., 2021).

The Beginning of the End

I retired in 1996 after serving over 15 years in the United States Army. First, I served in three Light Infantry Divisions and then was sent to the Field Artillery Training Center and Fort Sill, OK, until I retired. During my military service, civilian education became essential to achieving promotion points as an enlisted personnel. Due to this need, education centers became increasingly available on base.

Early in my military career, these centers encouraged me to utilize the Veterans Education Assistance Program (VEAP) benefits available to me to take classes. These are not meant to be confused with completing a degree program at an academic institution, but rather to facilitate the acquisition of skills and knowledge, ultimately to earn promotion points. Encouraging enrollment and completion of a degree program came later in my career, around 1987, if memory serves. During the early 1990s, earning a degree became increasingly necessary for a soldier to be promoted to the rank of E-6. With the reduction of forces during the mid-1990s, promotions were slow to come, and civilian education points were considered essential in achieving the necessary points to be promoted.

Out-Processing

My last days in the military consisted of attending morning accountability and then being released to conduct "retirement transition activities" before being out-processed. I believe it was called ACAP. I don't remember how many days it was, but I believe it was 15. I could be wrong; it was in the 20th century.

I was allowed to go to the career center and, yep, you guessed it! - construct a resume. During this transition phase, there was no assistance in translating military terms to civilian equivalents. This made it difficult because I didn't know how to indicate my qualifications on my resume. What I needed was more information about career networking and job placement services. This assistance should have been provided to all separating service members to facilitate effective transitions into the civilian workforce or to pursue further education.

Our education center had close ties to Cameron University (CU) and offered counselors to assist in enrolling in education benefits. However, I still had to do most of my processing on campus. The center could get everything rolling, but it all had to be finished on Cameron University's main campus.

My education benefits were from the Vietnam Era, VEAP. I would put in $1.00, which would get matched 2:1. My $1.00 became $3.00. I used that program in the military, and by the time I enrolled in CU, I had used up all my education benefits. When I retired, I had to cash in my share. The VEAP was only available to active-duty personnel. I only had a few hundred dollars in my account, so I received my portion still in my account when I retired.

As part of my ACAP, I was processed for a resume; I was given an appointment to explore enrollment in CU; I was given an appointment to see a "job assistance" counselor, they cancelled the appointment and could not reschedule; and I was given the point of contact information to schedule my retirement physical. Oh, by the way, I should have tried to schedule the physical the year before. The "wait list" for the physical varied from 9 to 10 months. So, I never received a retirement physical. That would hurt me later when applying for my VA benefits, but I digress.

Insufficient or inadequate resources supported my transition to retirement during the late 1990s. I retired from the US Army as an SGT, an E-5. For some reason, I was never "eligible" to pin on SSG or E-6 whenever I picked it up. Yes, one time was my fault. The other times were all internal politics, but that's another story for a different time and place.

During my ACAP process, I was told, off the record, that if I were a senior NCO or an LTC or above, I would have been a higher priority. I thought if I were a 1SG, MSG, SGM, or a COL or above when I retired, then I might have been "squeezed" in. It was not my imagination. Unfortunately, this practice is also reflected in the literature. It was important to note that participants who left the military in the higher ranks generally had positive transition experiences (Gordon et al., 2020). Both officers and veterans who had reached retirement age reported better transitioning outcomes. Those in the lower ranks reported more significant transition challenges, including junior NCOs. Medically discharged veterans also reported more substantial transition challenges (Rose et al., 2018).

I was an SGT. I retired from the U.S. Army as an SGT, an E-5. As I already mentioned, I was never "eligible" to pin on SSG or E-6 whenever I picked it up. Yes, one time was my fault. The other times were all internal politics, but that's another story for a different time and place. I was not worth their effort, in my opinion. An example of this is when my name was omitted from the program for my retirement ceremony. Yes, I felt hurt and betrayed. After serving my country, I was leaving the Army. I did not feel like I mattered; that feeling set upon me as I began to ACAP, and it hit home when I saw I was left out of the printed program.

These feelings are common among veterans upon separation. One life has ended, and our role has changed. I was transitioning from active duty to retirement as a US Army veteran. As did most of us, I faced many issues and demons.

Family

Those last few months of active duty were interesting. I realized my wife was having an affair with my squad leader. I suspected that my unit was aware of the affair, which was unfortunately confirmed later. A few months after retirement, our divorce was final. It was three months later that my ex-wife married my squad leader.

Looking back on thoughts about life after retirement, the plan was for me to be the "house-husband" until our son went to school. That would be another two years. At that time, we thought that my staying home with our son would be more beneficial than my working to pay for daycare, which would leave our son in non-family care. This plan changed when I found myself alone, no family, only me and my animals.

My challenges did ease over time; however, it was rough before it was better. In addition to a divorce, my stressors included filing for bankruptcy, financial troubles, and spending time incarcerated.

To ensure that student veterans transition to college and achieve academic success, family and social support play a crucial role; however, other resources are also available. There has been a shift in the type and amount of support services available for student veterans (Kirchner, 2015).

Transitioning to the civilian world and reintegrating into society while pursuing a degree may be one of the most challenging barriers a student veteran faces during their return to civilian life. Shifting from a structured military lifestyle to a less structured academic environment may be difficult (Godier-McBard et al., 2021; Kirchner, 2015). The difficulties I encountered were novel to me, yet they are shared experiences among veterans.

Fifty-two percent of student-veterans reported having dependents, compared to 20% of traditional students. Forty-five percent of the student-veterans reported being married, and 46% reported working part-time or full-time while attending school. Over 50% of student-veterans have a VA disability rating, with four out of five stating their disability contributes to their stress related to school (Stahley et al., 2022).

Financial

Can you guess what came after the trauma of divorce? Financial difficulties were next on the docket for me. As the sole provider with my retirement income, it was challenging to manage all the bills and mortgage payments on my own. While struggling to find my footing, I was then contacted and ordered to pay child support. While not included in the original parenting plan in the divorce decree, she later decided that she wanted this, despite stating during the divorce process that she did not want the money.

With my retirement, I made too much money to qualify for public assistance, so I picked up a part-time job. No, I didn't end up keeping it for long, but this challenge of finding employment for transitioning veterans is crucial.

In addition to ACAP activities, the stress of my family and financial issues created added stress to my life, in turn compounding my issues with mental health.

Substance Use

During my time in the military, I came to like pills, especially pain meds and prescription muscle relaxers. I remember I was unloading a pair of column speakers off a truck, one in each hand. The right went up on my shoulder with no problem, after all, I had done this numerous times. The left was not so cooperative. I felt a slight sharp pain and then numbness. I heard what sounded like a rip in a fabric; it was the muscle separating from the shoulder. My left arm went limp. I had pain in my neck, the C-4 vertebra, in my left shoulder, and across my trapezius muscles. I was taken to sick call and was provided a neck brace, a handout, and instructed in some physical therapy. I was also prescribed painkillers and muscle relaxers.

I remember not wanting to wait after asking for help getting a small airmobile tent out of the truck and to the location where it would be set up. We were participating in an exercise setting up the Tactical Operations Center (TOC). It was our unit, members of "Triple-deuce" and some MPs. I asked for help offloading a tent. I was asked what the matter was, why I couldn't carry it myself, and if I was too short or too weak to handle it.

After being accused of being too small or too weak, eventually, I put the tent on my back, holding the top of the bundle over my head and the straps in my arms. My arms were extended, so my elbows had a slight bend, keeping the bundle as high on my back as possible.

All anyone saw was a walking tent with only my legs visible. When I reached the target area, I stood up and tossed the tent a little behind me. Gravity did the rest. Thud. After asking for and not receiving help, it was where it needed to be. The tent was ready to be unwrapped and unfolded. This type of activity was common. As a side note, my stubbornness was noticed, and those who were "being lazy" were being motivated by a few senior NCOs. I think the sight of a "small" Army bandsman showing up the infantry got their senior NCOs' attention. We set up the TOC and our area quickly, once everyone was motivated.

The prescription medications often had me in a "purple haze" during road marches or field activities. I'd walk for miles and not remember how I got there. I remember walking, but the journey was just fuzzy in my mind. During the mundane and routine tasks, I would notice my mind wandering. Repetitive tasks didn't require "active" thinking skills. So, I went through the motions, just going through the motions.

There was one time in particular that I remember changing my socks at the top of Kole Kole Pass. I sat and admired the view, thinking, "This view is terrific!" It did not seem like time had passed until the sun rose for the return walk to the garrison. I was refreshed with water, clean socks, and I saw the glorious sunrise.

On a side note, I enjoyed my walks and runs up and down the pass. My times running the Kole Kole Half-marathon or walking up and down the pass with a ruck were worth it.

In Riggs et al. (2020), 7.4% of veterans reported an overdose in the last three years; 4.6% reported an overdose involving drugs, including 1.7% who reported overdosing on opioids. Overdoses involving alcohol were reported by 3.7% of veterans (Riggs et al., 2020). I was familiar with the dangers. With the help of a friend in the medical field, I formulated a plan to address pain management in holistic methodologies, stretching, and physical therapy. I have been "clean" for over 25 years.

Substance use or abuse was identified as a barrier to successful transitioning to the civilian world. Other issues identified included brain injury, suicide, mental health, and employment/unemployment (Ainspan et al., 2018; Godier-McBard et al., 2021). Rates for alcohol use have been reported to be 88.6% (one or more drinks in the last year) and 11.4% for illegal drugs. The opioid prescription rate was reported to have been 16.1% in 2016 as compared to the previous year, where alcohol consumption was reported at 81%, prescribed opioids were at 42%, tobacco was at 38%, marijuana was at 14%, and illegal drug use was listed at 2% (Bond et al., 2020).

Of the four studies that examined opioid use disorder treatment, one study found that veterans who received treatment had better outcomes than veterans who were untreated in the criminal justice system. Two studies found that illegal problems and activity decreased from the time of treatment admission to their follow-up. The last study also found veterans who stayed in treatment achieved better results than those who discontinued treatment. Longer treatments were associated with a lower likelihood of arrest after completion of the treatment plan (Timko et al., 2020). The VA plays an essential role in providing resources and addressing veterans' needs; however, 39% of veterans do not access VA health care. Of those who do, nearly one-third drop out after being diagnosed but not receiving treatment (Bond et al., 2020).

Homelessness

Finding housing that was not only affordable but also available proved to be a stressful situation for me. While waiting for an apartment to become available, I spent time living out of my van. Items that wouldn't fit in my van were stored, animals included. These additional costs made living in my van financially equivalent to paying rent. However, I felt lucky. I could sleep in my vehicle, protected from the weather. I worried about being hassled by the police, and I moved on when given a chance, which was most of the time, thankfully.

Homelessness is a significant concern for veterans. Without a consistent place to live, from which to receive mail, I encountered additional inconveniences beyond those of where to shower, dress, eat, and conduct daily activities. The concern of homelessness extends to financial difficulties, as filling out job applications was impossible. Employers do not accept applications without a home address. I remember putting "mobile" as my address on several job applications. Upon turning them in, I was asked for a "real address" to put on the application. Embarrassed, I explained my situation, and I was told to come back when I had a place to live. This stigma and societal norm are still in use today, with applications globally.

Homelessness is a significant public health problem in the United States, particularly among veterans (Crone et al., 2022; Nichter et al., 2023). Most health service conceptual models excluded homeless populations, focusing only on the general population's needs, the healthy, and the housed. The conceptual model of no health service access focuses explicitly on homeless veterans and the health services they use (Crone et al., 2022).

Nichter et al. (2023) listed the sociodemographic characteristics, military service characteristics, psychiatric characteristics, and psychological characteristics of veterans who experience homelessness. Many are divorced, lower-income, unemployed males who served voluntarily and received an other-than-honorable discharge. These individuals have TBI, PTSD, depression, or substance use, and fit most, if not all, of the characteristics (Nichter et al., 2023).

Housing stability remains crucial for enhancing quality of life, accessing health services, and meeting health needs. Colocation of services involves placing homeless and medical services in the same physical place (Crone et al., 2022). The homeless population usually walks as a primary mode of transportation. Facilities located near or at the homeless population's encampment encourage usage of the services provided at that location (health, dental, mental health, hearing, etc.). It is easier to access a facility nearby than it is to find transportation to a facility located miles away. Enrolling in primary health care is a gateway to other health services for many homeless veterans (Crone et al., 2022).

Research found low usage of clinical video visits among homeless veterans receiving a VA tablet. The physical or cognitive effects of having a substance use disorder further reduce the likelihood of visits. Homeless veterans are a priority of the VA, who face high rates of mental illness, suicide, and substance use disorder (Garvin et al., 2023).

Mental Health

As you can tell, many dynamics were screaming at me to get my stuff together. I started my road to "recovery" in 2012. I spent 20 minutes talking with a psychiatrist. After my visit, I was told to "Come back next year for a tune-up." I have been getting "tuned up" ever since. When I moved to Tennessee, to a new VA health care region, I was finally able to start my mental health maintenance in late 2016 at the local VA clinic. I have my "maintenance" appointments to keep me on track.

Ainspan et al. (2018) identified mental health as one of the many barriers to successfully transitioning from the military lifestyle to the civilian lifestyle. The researchers found that most treatment plans focus on symptom improvement rather than the veteran's daily life functioning. The VA is making strides to improve in this area by adopting a more holistic approach to healthcare, including mental healthcare. The Circle of Health, found at www.va.gov/wholehealth, is one such initiative.

Access to healthcare and services, as well as the rejection of the diagnosis, were common themes identified among veterans in Gordon et al. (2020). It was also common to hear from veterans that appointments often have long waiting times to get into a VA facility. Usually, the VA did not have available mental health appointments. In those cases, the veteran was provided with the VA Community Care Network (CCN) number. This sometimes involved several phone calls to coordinate services if CCN was available.

For me, mental health was available at the local clinic; however, after a few years, I needed to change doctors. I had to make an appointment with my primary care provider and explain why I wanted to go to CCN for mental health. Once the referral was approved, I contacted the CCN. They contacted a provider and called me. I then called the provider to confirm my appointment. At my VA clinic, eye exams are provided via the CNN. There is a glasses shop, but it does not offer exam capabilities. One phone number schedules me for an eye clinic appointment. I informed the representative at the eye clinic of my preference, and they authorized me for the services. I made the actual appointment day and time with the clinic.

For a healthcare specialist (e.g., hearing, eye, dental, OBGYN, mental health, gastrointestinal), coordination between the VA and the CCN clinic may vary. Some referrals to a CCN provider may require verification that the service is not available via the VA in the veteran's area, or validation and substantiated reasons why the veteran should be allowed to seek services outside of the VA system. This type of scenario may require additional exams or tests by the primary care physician to support the veteran's request. CNN network and services can be found at each local VA clinic or hospital, or by visiting www.va.gov/resources/about-our-va-community-care-network-and-covered-services/. The VA is expanding the reach of CCN facilities into rural areas to better provide care to those who do not have a VA facility within their geographical area.

Using primary healthcare data reported by Finnegan and Randles (2023), the following were the percentages of disorder prevalence in the veterans: Depression was accounted for in 18% of the population, alcohol misuse (17%), anxiety disorder (15%), PTSD (3%), and dementia at 2%. Thirty-eight percent of veterans' medical records were coded with a common mental condition. Mental health and well-being are closely tied to one's identity. The loss of identity creates a vulnerability to mental health symptoms as well as exacerbating symptoms (Gordon et al., 2020).

Disorder	Prevalence (%)
Depression	18%
Alcohol misuse	17%
Anxiety disorder	15%
PTSD	3%
Dementia	2%
Common mental condition	38%

Legal Matters

Sometime after 2012, a friend of mine and I were riding in the car. While we each had well-trimmed beards and donned hats identifying our military branch of service, the police officer decided to detain us because we looked like hippies, as if we smoked pot. We should not have been pulled over. The K-9 unit arrived, and the Supervisor came out. The additional officers lightly searched us and the car as the Supervisor asked what was going on. We were then allowed to continue on our way.

Another time I felt "targeted" by the police was during an episode when they were searching for someone who couldn't be located by the local authorities. I had fallen asleep on the bed reading Great Expectations when some acquaintances stopped by the house.

It just happened that the person the police were looking for had been outside my house in the alley before he took off. Even though the person never stepped into my home, I was taken to jail for interfering with their investigation and sheltering a person of interest. Sweet. I didn't have any plans for that day. What sucked was that I got to jail after lunch, and I was hungry and hadn't had any coffee. Suffice it to say, I was not happy.

In a systemic review of the literature on legal involvement after substance use and mental health treatment, Timko et al. (2020) found that almost one-third, 31.1%, of respondents had been arrested and booked. This rate is higher than that of civilians, 18.0%. Veterans of the All-Volunteer Force, post-1973, were more likely to be incarcerated than civilians and veterans who served during the draft era. The researchers concluded that substance use, mental health disorders, and criminal activity could be viewed as relapsing conditions that require ongoing support after treatment to maintain the treatment goals and prevent relapses (Timko et al., 2020).

Generally, veterans who receive treatment show improvement in criminal behavior outcomes from pre- to post-treatment. More sustained treatment was associated with better outcomes. Of the four studies that examined mental health treatment, all reported a decrease in legal problem severity or violence ideation from pre- to post-treatment. For veterans with co-occurring mental health and substance use disorders, the rates of criminal charges decreased when the VA provided treatment. VA may provide the organization and culture that veterans need to enhance treatment effectiveness (Timko et al., 2020).

Exit Services Upon ETS/Retirement (then)

My ACAP experience, my transition out of the military, was not the best; my rank didn't help. When I retired, one's rank determined a lot, especially the amount and quality of services offered to you. Education centers were beginning to become common on military bases. The training and education programs available today have evolved in response to the changing needs of our veterans.

Vocational training, retraining, and vocational rehabilitation programs were in their infancy during my transition. The 21st century has brought growth and development to the Transition Assistance Program's (TAP) services. Barriers to a positive transition experience still exist; however, the DoD, the VA, and veterans at large are identifying and addressing these barriers.

Chapter 3

Other Obstacles to Transitioning

Veterans often feel they cannot understand what we have experienced without a common frame of reference. A commonality of experiences facilitates a connection; the perceived lack of the same facilitates alienation, misunderstanding, and misperceptions about veterans. Unsupportive institutions, such as within the Department of Veterans Affairs (VA) system of facilities or places of employment, or a lack of support from the military service for transitioning, were a shared experience among veterans (Ahern et al., 2015; Burke, 2023, 2022b, 2021).

Sources

The barriers student veterans face, such as academic preparedness, confidence, understanding of the VA system and procedures, physical disabilities, and neurological concerns, such as traumatic brain injury (TBI) or post-traumatic stress disorder (PTSD), may hinder them from academic success (Ziencik, 2020). Proper support systems facilitate successful transitioning to academic success and civilian life. Barriers also include access and availability of VA facilities, financial and employment concerns, civilian misunderstanding of military culture, and the veteran's housing arrangements (Burke, 2024, 2023; Gavin et al., 2023; Le Page, 2020).

Student veterans often do not identify themselves as veterans in the classroom and are not easily identifiable among the student population; instead, they often identify as nontraditional students. Student veterans do not always mention VA appointments or medical needs. Veterans often separate themselves from the rest of the class (sitting in the back of the room, in a corner, or elsewhere) and speak only when spoken to. Not feeling welcome or accepted in the classroom hinders the transition to academic life (Blackwell-Starnes, 2018).

In Whitworth et al. (2020), 40 to 75% of participants described difficulties transitioning to civilian life. These difficulties included adjusting to work or education settings, substance abuse, finances, legal issues, family problems, and PTSD. Sixty percent of these service members stated that navigating the VA system for programs and benefits was difficult. Some veterans reported not knowing which agency or program to contact for assistance.

Employment

Transitioning from the military to civilian life is stressful for veterans, especially for those with service-connected disabilities seeking civilian employment (Bond et al., 2022). Employment in the wrong job, a hostile work environment, and unemployment hinder a successful transition to civilian life. Employment that does not fulfill the veteran's sense of purpose or is inadequate to support their family contributes to stress, relationship problems, and further mental health concerns (Ainspan et al., 2018). This information resonates with me as I reflect on the jobs I had with little to no meaning or fulfillment, and as a result, I couldn't keep those jobs for long. I also noticed that, during these times, my mental health, my self-worth, and my motivation were lacking.

PTSD has been connected to loss of employment, social isolation, impaired occupational functioning, suicide ideation, and potential for substance use. Veterans diagnosed with PTSD vary by service area, but it is estimated that 11-20% of veterans who served in Operation Iraqi Freedom or Operation Enduring Freedom have PTSD. Research findings revealed PTSD has a strong negative correlation to work outcomes, such as obtaining and maintaining employment (Shields et al., 2020).

Perkins et al. (2023) identified standard components among employment programs that veterans have identified. The most common content included career planning and exploration (61%), resume writing (59%), interview skills (35%), and translation of military skills (34%). Other components used included job training and certification (22%), entrepreneurship (18%), career fairs (17%), virtual career fairs (10%), or networking conferences (9%).

Component	Percentage
Career planning and exploration	61
Resume writing	59
Interview skills	35
Translation of military skills	34
Job training and certification	22
Entrepreneurship	18
Career fairs	17
Virtual career fairs	10
Networking conferences	9

Finances

Nearly one-third of post-9/11 veterans reported financial trouble in the last year, roughly twice the rate for pre-9/11 era veterans (Bond et al., 2020). Financial concerns, including the lack of a consistent paycheck and a guaranteed income, were significant considerations and burdens during the transition (Shue et al., 2021). Often, an occupation helps shape an identity. This sense of identity from our career leads to a renewed sense of purpose and, frequently, some level of career satisfaction.

Lee et al. (2020) discussed the barriers to transition that veterans face. The top two barriers listed were being financially prepared and finding employment. Other barriers included finding educational opportunities, relocation, health care, understanding VA benefits, and losing their veteran identity. In Maguire et al. (2022), 31.7% of veterans were not in a paid employment position, and 7.2% were not receiving any income.

Neurological Concerns

PTSD, TBI, depression, social anxiety, and other neurological concerns are often the most significant barriers; these internal battles, often silently endured by veterans, have a heavy impact. Clinicians and researchers must collaborate with veterans to design and develop new treatment methodologies and techniques to reduce the symptoms of military service, such as substance use and abuse, suicide, depression, PTSD, homelessness, and their loss of a sense of purpose as veterans transition from the military to civilian life and environment (Ainspan et al., 2018).

Veterans often interact with individuals who "treat PTSD as a joke." This misunderstanding increases the challenges in their transition (Morris et al., 2019). Research on the transition period from the military to civilian life is limited and has not adequately documented the scope of behavioral health or physical health problems among transitioning veterans or those who are at high risk for behavioral health or neurological problems (Bond et al., 2020; Godier-McBard et al., 2021).

The prevalence of PTSD and TBI has increased exponentially and resulted in devastating impacts on military personnel and their families, often requiring extensive rehabilitation. Common referrals for music therapy include PTSD and TBI treatment. This led to a more practical approach for veterans to receive clinical services via the VA (Vaudreuil et al., 2022).

Suicide Risk

Rates of suicide have increased since the early 2000s. The hazard rate of suicide is 2.5 times higher for veterans within their first year after separation from the military than for the active duty population. Veterans who are male, younger, with two years or less in military service, or who were separated from the Marine Corps or US Army had a higher risk of suicide during the first year of transitioning to civilian life (Ravindran et al., 2020). Mental health hygiene and maintenance, or lack thereof, play a significant factor in contemplating suicide.

Social disruptions, relationship dissolutions, financial insecurity, and legal issues are known precursor events and conditions that lead to suicidal ideation and acts of suicidal behavior. When creating a treatment plan, healthcare providers should inquire about social determinants of health (SDH) and consider these factors in their approach. Veterans' SDH data should be included in their electronic health records; this could improve suicide prevention (Blosnich et al., 2020).

Firearms are the most common method of suicide among veterans, although there is a higher percentage of men (70.2%) than women (49.8%). Women veterans are more likely to use a firearm to commit suicide than their civilian counterparts (Monteith et al., 2022). Suicidal ideation, firearm access, and preparatory behaviors were associated with acute (within 30 days) and chronic (within 365 days) suicide risk (Saulnier et al., 2025). Veteran women are more likely (26.3%) to use poison than male veterans (7.5%). The use of suffocation, 20.5% of veteran women vs. 16.8% of veteran men, and other methods (3.4% of veteran women vs. 5.5% of veteran men) is similar by gender (Monteith et al., 2022).

Study	Findings	Reference
Veteran women vs. men	Veteran women are more likely to use poison (26.3%) than male veterans (7.5%)	Monteith et al., 2022
Use of suffocation	20.5% of veteran women vs. 16.8% of veteran men	Monteith et al., 2022
Use of other methods	3.4% of veteran women vs. 5.5% of veteran men	Monteith et al., 2022

Suicide rates among veterans increased by 76.3% from 2001 to 2021. Suicide prevention is a top clinical priority of the VA (Saulnier et al., 2025). Veterans with higher social connectedness have been associated with lower PTSD symptom severity and suicidal rates (Flack & Kite, 2021).

Stigmas

Hearing peers or respected mentors admit to their struggles made other veterans feel more comfortable. This created an openness to discussing demons and coping mechanisms, leading to additional resources (Rose et al., 2018). Veterans bond with and talk to other veterans; they often feel that civilians lack an understanding of military culture.

Veterans identified several types of stigmas: internalized stigma, a veteran's negative impressions of seeking treatment and feeling ashamed; anticipated stigma, what veterans expect others to think about the veteran, being uncomfortable around the veteran or fearing the veteran; and public stigma, the general perception that the veteran is damaged or broken (Randles & Finnegan, 2021). Veterans believe dispelling the stigmas of mental health will help normalize help-seeking behavior. Veterans who recognized their mental health concerns were more than seven and a half times more likely to be receptive to help (Randles & Finnegan, 2021).

Mental health issues have been stigmatized within the military. As a result of this stigmatism, veterans may not report to clinics for treatment or may not report or underreport their mental health concerns. Have you ever been threatened with Non-Judicial punishment for going to Sick Call? That tends to make you less likely to seek treatment.

"Veteran as Borg?" The first time I recall thinking this was when Star Trek: First Contact was released in theaters—yes, theaters. After the movie, I overheard a child comment that someone exiting the venue looked like a Borg. I was proud of their parents' response. They explained the veteran lost an arm while serving our country. Of course, wearing his black hat distinguished him as a veteran. You have to love those black hats!

Let me put things in context. The veteran lost an arm and had a prosthetic replacement. Prosthetics of that time often looked intimidating. Technology has improved since the 1990s. Prosthetics are now designed and built to blend in with the body, being both aesthetically functional and unobtrusive. This brings us back to the Borg.

The Borg collective shares one mind; they think the same thoughts. They act only for the collective good. They assimilate everything they feel will improve the collective. The drones are implanted with cybernetic devices, such as eyes or arms, which serve a function for the drone. These devices often look bulky or oversized.

These prosthetic devices technologically augment the drone's capabilities, including eyesight, light frequencies, targeting, and assimilation tubes. These perceptions are also attached to veterans, that veterans are technologically augmented. Sometimes, they are seen as part robots.

Veterans are trained to think and act as a unit to complete their assigned mission. They are also expected to think for themselves and to act as the situation warrants, especially when changes need to be made, sometimes unexpectedly. While serving, veterans wear and/or carry their weapon systems and equipment, unlike the Borg. However, when fully geared up, it does look intimidating.

Veterans share an indelible life; it will never be taken away from us. Our everyday lives are shared; however, our individual circumstances make our lives unique. Our individuality is maintained. We are brothers and sisters. We are a collective, non-Borg.

I say non-Borg because veterans are individuals with feelings and life experiences. We are different from civilians and are often stigmatized as broken, unfeeling, unemotional, and prone to being violent at the drop of a hat. Veterans are human and have empathy and compassion. We have experiences to share.

At CU, I was setting up for a concert band rehearsal when I overheard a trumpet player tell another trumpet player they couldn't believe I could show such compassion. The trumpet player referred to a previous conversation I had with them about a death in their family. Being stigmatized and stereotyped negatively is a barrier to veterans transitioning to the civilian world. It makes forming positive relationships difficult.

Lack of "Reciprocal" Credentials

During my time in the military, I received many certifications. As an 88M/64C, I was qualified for anything with wheels and a trailer. With my Hazardous Materials Handler and Inspector certifications from the U.S. Army and the U.S. Air Force, I could have found a nice job. I would have made even more money by combining the two areas. However, it was easier said than done to transition out of the service and into civilian life, securing employment in the private sector where I could utilize the skills I had honed over my years of service. It occurred to me decades later what my ex-wife meant when she said I was not "ambitious enough." I never did fulfil my role as a civilian in a career with an equivalent skill set to the one I used during my military service.

I secured positions in the education field. After receiving my teaching license from the state of Oklahoma, I relocated to Tennessee. My certification was transferred, and I only had to pay a license fee to secure my license in my new state of residence. In this case, there was reciprocity for credentialing between Oklahoma and Tennessee. Some states would not accept my out-of-state license, and I would be required to take certification classes and pass their specific state tests to obtain a license. Then, I would have to pay the additional license fee. Clinicians, educators, lawyers, and other professionals should verify the existence of "reciprocity" agreements when transferring their specific discipline credentials to a new area.

Skills Translation- Resume vs. Skills List, Translation

Veterans reported finding no acknowledgment of their prior accomplishments and little to no transferability of skills developed in the military (Gordon et al., 2020). Military occupations may not translate to civilian occupations (Morgan et al., 2020).

Organizations offering veteran services that assist in the translation of skills from service to post-service careers include: the Military Skills Translator, include Military.com, CareerOneStop, and O*NET OnLine. These tools translate most job skills but lack information on non-technical skills and identify employment opportunities (Jim-Suleiman et al., 2021). The effective translation of military skills to employment goes beyond the technical job skills translator software.

LePage's (2020) recommendations encompass two areas, informed by the findings and guided by the theoretical lens. The first area was hiring and training, which included job skills matching, clearly stated expectations and standards, and a clear understanding of veteran health issues and disability laws. The second area was supportive policies and practices, which include social and peer support, as well as supportive leadership. Veterans often leave their civilian jobs frequently, with 50% of them leaving within their first year of employment.

Veterans are not only seeking stable and challenging employment, but they also often require it to make successful contributions to society. Employment is often viewed as a way of life for veterans, an integral part of their self-identity. Their passion for discipline is often part of their self-identity as well. When skills do not translate to the civilian world or the job does not align with their long-term goals, veterans often find alternative employment (LePage, 2020).

Job/Career/Unemployment

Transportation and access to childcare are concerns for veterans with children as they transition to the civilian workforce. Having both dependable transportation and childcare relieves pressure on the family dynamic. When reliable childcare is found, the concerns of affordability and caretaker competency become additional focuses. If the VA were to provide childcare services, veterans and their families would use them (Morgan et al., 2020).

Rates of PTSD among post-9/11 veterans typically average between 5 and 15%, and depression rates range from 2 to 10% compared to 2.6% and 5.2% in the general U.S. population. TBI has been diagnosed in 8% of post 9/11 veterans. These conditions, as well as standard physical injuries reported by veterans, including chronic pain, back problems, and limb amputations, pose barriers for veterans seeking employment (Perkins et al., 2023).

Veterans who obtain and retain employment have an easier time transitioning. Organizations should provide veterans with clear performance standards so they understand the organization's performance expectations, parameters, and processes. Veterans are affected by their social/peer support, the culture, and their environment. Supportive workplace services that promote peer support may help mitigate transition issues resulting from a lack of supportive relationships (LePage, 2020).

Education

As non-traditional students, veterans enter the academic world with more skills than an entry-level freshman. Veteran students are also often older than the traditional student arriving from high school. Identifying with persons in the scholarly community, in addition to the students, is complex, often due to differences in age and experience. Veterans perceive that civilians do not understand the military way of life and what they experience while in uniform. Developing a sense of belonging and community facilitates transitioning from military to academic life (Blackwell-Starnes, 2018). I found the brotherhood of the Zeta Tau chapter of Kappa Kappa Psi as my venue to "belong." Actually, they found me.

Those with lower education levels who have not progressed to college are more likely to identify as veterans (63.5% vs 45.5%). A veteran's identity is shaped by their experience transitioning out of the military, as they form a new identity in response to the feelings of isolation and connectedness they experience after discharge (Dolan et al., 2022).

Compared to their traditional student counterparts, older veterans usually have a wider age gap than veterans who have served only one tour of duty. This age gap, or generation gap, is often challenging to overcome (Morris et al., 2019).

Availability

The availability or lack of availability of VA facilities or appointments, as well as a lack of assistance with obtaining VA benefits, determining eligibility for benefits, and applying for benefits, are barriers to a successful transition to the civilian world (Morgan et al.,

2020). VA and other veteran support agencies need to increase awareness of the various programs available to veterans and their families to help them obtain VA benefits. Almost one-third of veterans report utilizing at least one VA healthcare service. VA benefits are a primary concern for veterans transitioning to civilian life (Morgan et al., 2020).

Transportation, lack of available appointments, and staffing issues were indicated as barriers to accessibility to mental health treatment. Veterans prioritized their basic needs (such as housing and employment) over their mental health treatment. Homelessness also hinders access to services. Not having a place to function from, such as an address, a cell phone, or a regular contact point, adds to transition barriers (Randles & Finnegan, 2021).

In researching health services among homeless veterans, Crone et al. (2022) defined access as the opportunity, or ease, with which veterans may use appropriate services, including healthcare. The five dimensions of the Access Model include Availability (having a clinic or hospital close by), Accessibility (can the facility be easily traveled to and from?), Accommodation (meeting the needs of the veteran), Affordability, and Acceptability. These are interactions between the veteran and their clinician or health care system (Crone et al., 2022).

Four reviewed studies focused on two dimensions: Availability and Acceptance. Availability was paired with Accessibility in one study, and Accommodations were paired with Acceptance in another. Availability and Acceptance were mentioned most often in the literature addressing more than one barrier by dimension; however, Affordability had no mentions (Crone et al., 2022).

Academic Support

Academic support at administrative offices and veteran support centers impacts the transition of student-veterans. Veterans often lack guidance during registration or are unaware of the services available on campus. Advisors and other administrative offices within academic institutions (such as financial aid, enrollment, Academic Affairs, Student Services, etc.) need to ensure that staff are adequately trained to work specifically with student veterans. A veteran-specific orientation is recommended to facilitate the transition of veterans to academic life. Another recommendation is to train faculty and staff to understand the classroom needs of student veterans. (Blackwell-Starnes, 2018; LePage, 2020; Stahley et al., 2022).

The Office of Academic Affairs traditionally handles all aspects of the student's degree program, focusing on classes, scheduling, professors, and curriculum issues.

The Office of Student Services traditionally handles all aspects of the academic experience, except the student's degree program. Concerns addressed here include, but are not limited to, enrollment, on-campus transportation system, conflicts with administrative offices such as Financial Aid, VA Coordinator, Admissions, Enrollment, Benefits and Assistance Office (health insurance, and other "perks" offered at the institution), and the Housing Office. This office encompasses various aspects of academic life. The Office of Student Organizations handles all aspects of being an institutionally recognized student organization. Each institution has its own requirements to be an active student organization.

When discussing support services with student-veterans at past National Conferences (2024, 2023, and 2022) and Regional Summits (St. Louis, 2024), student-veterans stated that when the offices are fully staffed with properly trained and VA-certified personnel, they are more likely to have a positive experience transitioning to student-veterans. The human factor, which encompasses how the representative treats the veteran, includes work ethic, work performance, attitude, body language, student interaction, and other factors that influence support quality. Student-veterans stated that personal interactions played a big part in the VA process.

Many academic institutions have support organizations for veterans, veteran dependents, and veteran caregivers, often referred to as military-affiliated students. Chapter 4 discusses these support agencies.

Chapter 4

Available Resources to Facilitate Transitioning

Many of these resources were unavailable or did not exist when I transitioned out of the military and became a student-veteran. I am familiar with several organizations and resources mentioned in this chapter, including the VFW, the American Legion, and the SVA. However, my experiences with VSOs may differ from those of others. To that end, this chapter provides more information and less of a story on transition.

The 2025 Federal Benefits Guide for Veterans, Dependents, Survivors, and Caregivers provides information on benefits and services currently available by law and regulation. VA validated the information provided in the guide as of October 10, 2024. Please go to www.va.gov to access the latest updates on Veteran care and benefits.

The U.S. Department of Veterans Affairs, based on 38 U.S.C. § 101(2), defines a veteran as an individual who served in the active military, naval, or air service and was discharged or released therefrom under conditions other than dishonorable. The estimated number of veterans in 2019 was 18.3 million (Umucu, 2023).

Overall, 25% to 38% of all veterans reported difficulty adjusting to civilian life. Personal factors included demographic variables and health variables. The critical determinants of a successful transition included satisfying work (26.8% of respondents), stable mental health (20.0% of respondents), family support (18.9% of respondents), and a strong spousal relationship (16.8% of respondents). The transition would be smoother if civilians understood military life (28.4% of respondents), finances were a concern, veterans were worried they did not have enough money (28.4% of respondents), and having someone to talk with while transitioning (11.8% of respondents) completed the survey analysis (Rose et al., 2018).

Aspect	Percentage
Difficulty adjusting to civilian life	25% to 38%
Satisfying work	26.8%
Stable mental health	20.0%
Family	18.9%

Aspect	Percentage
Spousal relationships	16.8%
Civilians' understanding of military life	28.4%
Concern about finances	28.4%
Having someone to talk with	11.8%

Morris et al. (2019) listed sources of support found on campus. Those sources, listed from most frequent to least frequent, included campus veterans services, family and friends, professors, academic advisors, other veterans, disability services, military transition programs, campus wellness center, military transition courses, service animals/pets, and civilians. It is necessary to actively prepare for the transition to civilian life. There is a potential negative impact on one's psyche (Shue et al., 2021). My sources of support on campus were fraternal. Being a member of Kappa Kappa Psi helped me find my sense of identity as a student-veteran.

U.S. veterans frequently report difficulties transitioning from military to civilian life. The 4-S Transition Model identifies four key factors that influence the transition process: the situation, the self, support, and strategies. Veterans believed that preparation for the transition process was crucial to achieving success. Other factors affecting the career transition process included the feeling that the transition experience resulted in a loss of structure and the challenge of establishing oneself outside the military (Shue et al., 2021). My experience reaffirmed that a strong support system is essential for successfully transitioning from military to civilian life.

Transition services come in many forms and from various sources. Their availability varies by academic institution and geographical area. Services are less available in the more rural areas. The Veterans Integration to Academic Leadership (VITAL) Initiative increases access to resources and treatment via on-campus clinical services (McCaslin et al., 2014).

Department of Defense (DoD)/Service Branches

The Department of Defense (DoD) has seen 200,000 individuals leave the military annually in recent years and expects this trend to continue in the foreseeable future (Ainspan et al., 2018). Pre-release support services were identified as critical elements to facilitate a successful transition (Rose et al., 2018).

DoD- Transition Assistance Program (TAP)

The Military Personnel Transition Assistance Act of 1990 mandated the establishment of a transition assistance program for transitioning military personnel; each service developed its own version (Ziencik, 2020). The Transition Assistance Program (TAP) is mandatory for all service members exiting the military. TAP is focused on the elements of finding employment (Keeling, 2018). The TAP curriculum includes a model for potential entrepreneurs (Ainspan et al., 2018).

Military personnel are required to attend the TAP as provided by their service branch. The purpose was to provide transition services to veterans and their dependents for civilian life by offering information resources, tools, and training over a five-day period, with additional training provided between 12 and 24 months (Ziencik, 2020).

One investigation found that unemployed veterans using the TAP found employment three weeks sooner than those veterans who did not use the TAP (Perkins et al., 2023). However, only approximately 55% of separating service members leaving active duty participate. A supportive chain of command affects this utilization percentage. (LePage, 2020).

U.S. Department of Veterans Affairs (VA)

The Veterans Health Administration (VHA) is the largest healthcare system in the United States, serving over 8 million patients annually with more than 8 million employees. VHA addresses veterans' medical issues and is expected to acknowledge and respond to veterans' non-medical determinants of health (Blosnich et al., 2020).

VA offers numerous benefits to veterans. Most well-known are the benefits of education, health, and mental health. The VA may provide the organization and culture that veterans need to enhance their mental health treatment (Timko et al., 2020). VA also provides health care and non-health care benefits, such as benefits for disabled veterans, veteran readiness and employment, pension, education and training, home loans, life insurance, homelessness assistance and prevention, and burial and memorial benefits. A complete list may be found in the Federal Benefits for Veterans, Dependents, Survivors, and Caregivers, 2025 edition, Pamphlet 80-25-1.

This pamphlet outlines education benefits to assist veterans, service members, and qualifying dependents with needs such as funding college tuition, locating an academic institution or training program, and accessing career counseling (U.S. Department of Veterans Affairs, 2025).

VA- Transition Programs

The VA portion of the TAP is a one-day, in-person course titled "VA Benefits and Services." It helps veterans understand and navigate the VA, as well as the benefits and services they've earned. The course offers interactive exercises and real-world examples, covering family support, disability compensation, education, and healthcare benefits.

SkillBridge is a DoD program for transitioning service members offering employment training, internships, and apprenticeship opportunities at more than 3,000 public and private organizations nationwide. VA also offers SkillBridge opportunities for civilian careers.

WARTAC is a skill-based education and employment opportunity for wounded warriors and transitioning service members to complete a national-level Visual Basic Applications (VBA) training program while still on active duty. Participants learn the skill set of a Rating Veteran Service Representative (RVSR) or Veteran Service Representative (VSR).

VA Solid Start supports the transition from service and welcomes veterans to the VA. During the first year of their transition journey, the veteran receives three calls: 90, 180, and 365 days after separation.

Information on the VA Transition Programs may be found at https://discover.va.gov/transition-programs/.

VA- Health

Each veteran's medical benefits package is unique. Yours may include care and services to treat illnesses and injuries, prevent future health problems, improve your ability to function, and enhance quality of life. All veterans receive coverage for most care and services; some also qualify for additional benefits, such as dental care. LGBTQ+ veterans are eligible for the same VA benefits as any other veteran and will be treated in a welcoming environment. For more information on LGBTQ+ care, visit www.patientcare.va.gov/LGBT.

The complete list of covered benefits depends on your priority group, the advice of your VA primary care provider (doctor, nurse practitioner, or physician's assistant), and medical standards for treating any health conditions you may have. VA Health Benefits include all necessary inpatient hospital care and outpatient services to promote, preserve, or restore your health. VHA medical facilities offer a range of traditional hospital-based services, including surgery, critical care, mental health, orthopedics, pharmacy, radiology, and physical therapy. Information on VA Health may be found at www.va.gov/health-care/about-va-health-benefits/.

The webpage also provides information on vision, dental, assisted living, non-covered services, copays, prescription coverage (both in-network and out-of-network), interactions with Medicare, Medicaid, and other private insurance, as well as access to VA care facilities. Towards the bottom of the page is a link to Disability Compensation. Disability Compensation and the VA health system do not communicate with each other. One must file separately for each. Compensation information may be found at https://www.benefits.va.gov/compensation/index.asp.

Telehealth is the delivery of healthcare services when distance becomes a barrier to care. This includes exchanging and utilizing medical information and telecommunication technologies to promote long-distance care. Standard methods include video-conferencing, store-and-forward video or imaging, streaming, and wireless communication (Vaudreuil et al., 2022).

Due to the distance factor of telehealth, assessments must occur throughout the session. Patients should feel as safe with their telehealth appointments as they do with in-person treatment. Telehealth extends the therapeutic reach to bring care to patients in their homes or communities. A particular trust is established when patients invite therapists into their homes. (Vaudreuil et al., 2022).

Video telehealth visits through the VA Video Connect app allow homeless veterans to access clinical services. A systemic review found that mobile health intervention for prevention of alcohol and other substance use/abuse is practical and effective (Garvin et al., 2023). The VA Office of Rural Health and the VA Office of Connected Eye Care expanded video visits via the VA VIDEO Connect app. They initiated a nationwide tablet distribution effort to overcome access barriers experienced by low-income and rural veterans seeking care at VA facilities. An added benefit of the video visits is reduced isolation through connecting with VA providers (Garvin et al., 2023).

Telehealth and other technologies may introduce new ways to serve veterans (Tsai et al., 2022). The VA has adopted the Circle of Health, a holistic approach to treating veterans. This approach incorporates various aspects of healing, medicine, herbs, and the environment. The VA refers to it as the Circle of Health. The equation starts with the veteran, then adds "self-care," "professional care," and "community" to equal "Whole Health". This is similar to an equation I published in my dissertation, "Student-veteran + Support Services (on and near campus) for PTSD =

Academic Success/Life Success." My dissertation focused on PTSD support (Burke, 2021). I'm pleased to see this model coming to fruition. Information on Whole Health may be found at
https://www.va.gov/wholehealth/index.asp.

The Elizabeth Dole Home and Community-Based Services for Veterans and Caregivers Act of 2023, also known as the Elizabeth Dole Home Care Act, addresses the VA's home care and caregiver programs. Under this bill, the cost of providing noninstitutional alternatives to nursing home care may not exceed the cost incurred if a veteran were furnished with VA nursing home care.

Among other requirements, the VA must: establish a partnership with the Program of All-Inclusive Care for the Elderly in certain areas to furnish non-institutional alternatives to nursing home care; implement programs, such as the Veteran Directed Care Program, to expand access to home- and community-based services; provide specified support and benefits to caregivers of certain disabled veterans; implement a pilot program to provide homemaker and home health aide services to veterans who reside in communities with home health aide shortages; and ensure availability of home and community-based services for Native American veterans. A summary and information on this Act may be found at https://www.congress.gov/bill/118th-congress/senate-bill/141?q=%7B%22search%22%3A%22s.+141%22%7D&s=5&r=301.

VA- Mental Health

Several evidence-based counseling strategies exist to work with veterans with PTSD. They include trauma-based and non-trauma-based therapies, along with pharmacological methodologies. Tailoring a treatment plan to the individual ensures the most effective results.

Cognitive Behavioral Therapy (CBT) involves talking. CBT is a short-term, goal-oriented approach that focuses on problem-solving. CBT focuses on the individual's core beliefs at the root of the trauma and works to change the individual's attitudes and beliefs causing stress in their life (Shields et al., 2020).

Trauma-Focused Cognitive Behavioral Therapy (TF-CBT) is often the treatment of choice for those with PTSD. It modifies negative thoughts while changing the memory associated with the trauma, then removing problematic behavior related to the event. Clinician and client work together to determine the best treatment plan. Vivo exposure (therapy where veterans directly confront their demons) identifies activities, people, or places the client has avoided. Then, the client interacts with one of these. Imaginal exposure involves the client describing the trauma and reliving the experience in their imagination. The client identifies triggers associated with re-experiencing the event, then identifies how things are different now compared to the original event (Shields et al., 2020).

Other methodologies include Cognitive Reconstruction, Cognitive Processing Therapy, Eye Movement Desensitization and Reprocessing (EMDR), Prolonged Exposure (PE), and Psychodynamic Psychotherapy (Shields et al., 2020). Therapies that involve radical acceptance, immersion, or exposure therapy are often intense. The clinician and veteran must collaborate to develop the most effective treatment plan to achieve the desired treatment goals.

The VA offers various mental health resources, information, treatment options, and more—all accessible to veterans, their supporters, and the general public. Explore the pages cited below to learn more about a specific topic or find information tailored to your needs. You can also visit the "Get Help" page to explore VA resources that address the unique stressors and experiences veterans may face. Specific topics include, but are not limited to, anxiety, bipolar, depression, TBI, sexual trauma, PTSD, substance use, suicide, and more. They also offer resources in the following categories: transitioning service members, women veterans, LGBTQ+ veterans, older Veterans,

and more. There are links to various articles, literature, and updates on mental health issues. Information on VA Mental Health may be found at
https://www.mentalhealth.va.gov/.

VA- Support and Family Education (SAFE) Program

The VA mental health program consists of 14 sessions that involve family and a psychoeducational curriculum. It is a family education program for people who care for or about someone with a mental illness. Each session lasts 90 minutes and is held once a month. (Ainspan et al., 2018; Sherman, 2014). The SAFE Program includes one session focused on PTSD. Mental healthcare professionals facilitate the SAFE Program sessions. Information may be found at
https://pubmed.ncbi.nim.nih.gov/.

VA- Veterans Integration to Academic Life (VITAL) Initiative

The VA implemented the Veterans Integration to Academic Leadership (VITAL) Initiative in 2011 through the Veterans Health Administration (VHA). VITAL increases access to resources and treatment through on-campus clinical services and establishes connections between VA medical centers and academic settings (McCaslin et al., 2014). Such coordination would be welcome as an available resource, supported by the existing literature of Kinney et al. (2020), Kirchner & Biniecki (2019), and my own published research from 2021. Available support services for student veterans with PTSD facilitate academic success and a positive academic experience (Kirchner, 2015; Osborne, 2016; Young & Phillips, 2019). Long before this initiative, I was fortunate enough to attend campuses with such collaborations.

Currently, 21 VHA-administered VITAL Initiative sites collaborate with more than 105 campuses to provide high-quality healthcare and improve veterans' overall mental health, while supporting their transition to university campuses. This also includes raising awareness of VHA healthcare benefits and facilitating VHA enrollment, including links to VA specialty healthcare and mental health clinics, as well as coordinating with on-campus and community services and educating the campus community on the challenges facing student-veterans, among other initiatives (McCaslin et al., 2014). Enrollment in the VA health care benefits, coordination of campus services, and engagement with veteran-based student organizations are the best activities that the VITAL teams perform.

I found this information on a fact sheet dated March 11, 2025: Veterans Integration to Academic Leadership (VITAL) is a Veterans Health Administration (VHA) national program under Mental Health Services (MHS). VITAL operates in 23 medical centers across 16 Veterans Integrated Services Networks (VISNs). These facilities serve 100 colleges and universities across the nation. This number has increased by two since 2014, and it is expected to continue growing.

I sent an e-mail inquiring about the number of facilities, and I was provided with the website information, the "Locator" tab. I was instructed to click each location for a list of facilities, if available. I found a total of 163 academic institutions are covered: three academic institutions covered in Alabama, 13 in California, four in Colorado, five in Connecticut, five in Hawai'i, 20 in Illinois, one in Kansas, four in Maryland, seven in Massachusetts, 10 in Michigan, 17 in Minnesota, two in Missouri, four in Nevada, 10 in New Jersey, 22 in New York, one in North Dakota, three in Ohio, one Online, two in Pennsylvanian, four in South Carolina, nine in Texas, eight in Utah, five in Wisconsin, and three in Wyoming.

State	Number of Academic Institutions
Alabama	3
California	13

State	Number of Academic Institutions
Colorado	4
Connecticut	5
Hawai'i	5
Illinois	20
Kansas	1
Maryland	4
Massachusetts	7
Michigan	10
Minnesota	17
Missouri	2
Nevada	4
New Jersey	10
New York	22
North Dakota	1

State	Number of Academic Institutions
Ohio	3
Online	1
Pennsylvania	2
South Carolina	4
Texas	9
Utah	8
Wisconsin	5
Wyoming	3

You may find the VITAL website (with access to contact information for the VITAL team near you) at www.mentalhealth.va.gov/studentveteran/vital.asp.

VA- Homeless Patient Aligned Care Team (HPACT) Model

Tsai et al. (2022) conducted a narrative review of the HPACT model enacted by the VA in 2011. Healthcare for the homeless is often inadequate, with many studies finding high rates of acute healthcare utilization, lower rates of primary care, and poor-quality outcomes observed within the homeless veteran population. HPACT started with trial sites in 2011. Funding was increased in 2012 to accommodate 32 VA medical facilities, later expanded to more than 60 VA facilities. This increase highlights a shift from a "one-size-fits-all" to a more specialized treatment plan (Tsai et al., 2022).

The HPACT program serves more than 18,000 veterans annually, coming from diverse backgrounds, areas of service, and branches of service. The average patient was 53 years old, 4% were women, and 8.8% served after September 11, 2001. As they find housing, veterans in HPACT often transition to traditional VA primary care facilities (Tsai et al., 2022).

VA- Education and Training

The Post-9/11 GI Bill is an education benefit for those serving active duty after 10 September 2001. For more information, visit www.va.gov/education/about-gi-bill-benefits-9-11. To be eligible, a veteran must have served at least 90 days after 10 September 2001 or be honorably discharged. This includes service performed by National Guardsmen under Title 32 U.S.C. for recruiting, instruction, or training the National Guard or section 502(f) to respond to a national emergency.

Service members may receive up to 36 months of entitlement. No beneficiary may use more than 48 months of education and training benefits from any combination of programs except for the Veteran Readiness and Employment (VR&E) benefits. Approved training includes graduate and undergraduate degrees, vocational/technical training, on-the-job training and apprenticeships, flight training, correspondence training, licensing, national testing/credentialing programs, and tuition assistance.

If a veteran is eligible for the Montgomery GI Bill and qualifies for the Post-9/11 GI Bill, a selection process is in place to choose a program; however, changes in this area allow veterans to utilize benefits from both programs. Always check for the latest policy on this; time limits apply.

Tuition and fees are paid to the institution, which is responsible for refunding any overpayment to the student. A monthly housing allowance (MHA) is paid directly to the student, provided they attend more than half-time. MHA is currently equal to the basic allowance for housing for an E-5 with dependents, prorated based on the rate of pursuit (full-time, ¾-time, etc.) and benefit level. MHA is calculated based on the campus' Zip code, where students physically attend most classes. If students take online courses, their MHA is half the national average. MHA is not payable to those enrolled in flight school or correspondence training, individuals attending half-time or less, or active-duty members or their spouses. Current rates and eligibility requirements can be found at www.va.gov/education/benefits-rates.

The Yellow Ribbon GI Bill Education Enhancement Program allows institutions in the U.S. and overseas to voluntarily enter into an agreement with the VA to fund tuition and fees that exceed the amounts payable under the Post-9/11 GI Bill. The institution contributes a dollar amount, and the VA will match the contribution, not to exceed 50% of the difference. For more information, visit www.va.gov/education/about-gi-bill-benefits/post-9-11/yellow-ribbon-program.

The VA Federal Benefits for Veterans, Dependents, Survivors, and Caregivers 2025, Pamphlet 80-25-1, also lists and discusses the Marine Gunnery Sergeant John David Fry Scholarship and the Edith Nourse Rogers STEM Scholarship. The GST Fry Scholarship provides benefits to the children and surviving spouses of service members who died after 10 September 2001 while serving on active duty or who died from a service-connected disability while a member of the elected Reserve. The Edith Nourse Rogers STEM scholarship provides up to nine months of additional benefits (a maximum of $30,000). To be eligible, the veteran must have exhausted (or will exhaust their Post-9/11 GI Bill entitlements within 180 days) and complete at least 60 semester credit hours or 90 quarter hours toward their degree. Programs must have at least 120 semester credit hours or 180 quarter credit hours for completion, or they must be a teaching certification program.

Survivors and Dependents' Educational Assistance (DEA) offers education and training opportunities for dependents of veterans who (a) are permanently and totally disabled due to a service-related condition, or (b) died while on active duty as a result of a service-related condition. Dependents may be eligible for 36 or 45 months if benefits were used before 1 August 2018 for degree and certificate courses, apprenticeships, and on-the-job training. Surviving spouses lose eligibility if they remarry before the age of 57 or are living with another person who has been recognized publicly as their spouse. Dependent children do not lose eligibility if the surviving spouse remarries.

Visit www.va.gov/education/survivor-dependent-benefits/dependents-education-assistance for more information.

The Montgomery GI Bill Active Duty (MGIB-AD), known as Chapter 30, provides up to 36 months of education benefits for a college degree, certification programs, technical/vocational courses, flight training, apprenticeships or on-the-job training, high-tech training, licensing, and certification training, entrepreneurship training, specific entrance examinations, and correspondence courses. Benefits generally expire 10 years after discharge. Veterans may be eligible for this benefit if they entered active duty after 30 June 1985, are honorably discharged, did not decline MGIB in writing, and served three continuous periods of active duty or four years in the Selected Reserve after active duty service. Current payment rates are available at www.va.gov/education/about-gi-bill-benefits/montgomery-active-duty.

Additional non-VA resources may be found at https://www.benefits.va.gov/gibill/non_va_resources.asp. Links are provided in the following categories: Certifying Official Links, State Veterans Benefits, Federal Government Websites, Military Websites (Department Level), Financial Aid, Employment, and Miscellaneous.

To file online for education benefits, visit www.va.gov/education/how-to-apply. You may also visit your nearest VA regional office to apply in person. To find an office near you, go to www.benefits.va.gov/benefits/offices.asp. You may also consult with the VA certifying official at the registrar's or financial aid office. You may also call 888-GI BILL-1 (888-442-4551) or 800-MyVA411 (800-698-2411), option 5, to request that the form be mailed to you.

VA- Veteran Readiness & Employment (VR&E)

Veterans may receive Veteran Readiness and Employment (VR&E) services to help with job training, education, employment accommodation, resume development, and job-seeking skills coaching. Other services may be provided to assist Veterans and Service members in starting their own businesses or independent living services for those severely disabled and unable to work in traditional employment. VR&E was formerly known as Vocational Rehabilitation and Employment. For more information, visit https://www.benefits.va.gov/vocrehab/index.asp.

The VR&E program is now designated as Chapter 31. You must not have received a dishonorable discharge and must have a disability rating of at least 10% from the VA to be eligible. If you were discharged after January 1, 2013, there is no time limit on your eligibility. If you use VR&E benefits, the VA will not deduct entitlement from your other VA education benefits, like the Post-9/11 GI Bill or the Montgomery GI Bill.

Frequently asked questions and further information may be found at https://www.va.gov/careers-employment/vocational-rehabilitation/eligibility/.

Apply online or by U.S. mail. Please send your completed form to the Department of Veterans Affairs, VR&E Intake Center, P.O. Box 5210, Janesville, WI. 53547-5210. You may alternatively apply by visiting a VA Regional office and having a VA employee assist you. You may also have an accredited attorney, claims agent, or VSO (such as the VFW, Legion, DAV, PVA, or other VSO discussed in this chapter) to apply on your behalf. Instructions on how to apply may be found at https://www.va.gov/careers-employment/vocational-rehabilitation/how-to-apply/.

Civilian Organizations

The federal government is not the only source of support for veterans; numerous civilian VSOs and non-profit organizations aid veterans as they transition to the civilian world. Veterans often seek to belong and fit in. They don't always wish to be identified as a veteran, so an organization's environment influences the veteran's comfort and acceptance. Too much military memorabilia may project an image of a USO or recruitment office- too many identifiers for their comfort. The environment should reflect our military heritage and culture; however, it should make us feel as if we are transitioning from veterans to members of the civilian world. These organizations should project a hopeful future for veteran civilians.

Veterans Service Organization (VSO)

In addition to peer support options, engagement in VSOs can help address social isolation and improve the transition from military to civilian life. Such interactions can facilitate the application for VA benefits, which in turn can help identify and treat necessary issues. Timely treatment of our veterans is essential (Ainspan et al., 2018).

Student Veterans of America (SVA)

The SVA currently has over 1,600 chapters on campuses worldwide. It focuses on helping student veterans, dependents, and caregivers reach their full potential. The SVA is the premier organization that leads the way in research, service, and advocacy for veterans and military-affiliated students.

The SVA's mission is to catalyze student veteran success by providing resources, network support, and advocacy "to, through, and beyond" higher education. The SVA achieves this through various leadership, advocacy, and legislative programs that give student veterans a voice in Washington, D.C., provide access to VA benefits applications, offer transition services to help veterans transition to become student-veterans, and develop leadership skills.

The SVA Home page, located at https://studentveterans.org/, features SVA news, scholarships, programs, and events, including NatCon, regional summits, the Leadership Institute, and Washington Week. Scroll to the bottom of the page to find a chapter near you. SVA Headquarters is 655 15th Street NW, Suite 320, Washington, D.C. 20005. The view from the roof is breathtaking!

SVA- MySVA Portal

The MySVA portal is where you fill out your profile, access SVA programs, update chapter membership, and access APEX and Mental Health Resources. Everything is tailored specifically for you and your needs. The more information you provide in your profile, the more meaningful the resources. You'll find tabs with Announcements, Scholarships, access to the Basic Needs and Wellness Survey, plus My Success Hub.

SVA- My Success Hub

My Success Hub gives you access to the Advising Center, Programs and Events, Chapter Services, Resource Center, and the Career Center.

The Advising Center provides specialized and personalized academic coaching, tools, and support to transitioning service members, veterans, and their families. With early guidance, you can discover your path and optimize your educational benefits. For more information and resources, please visit https://studentveterans.org/success-hub/advising-center/. Logging in via the MySVA Portal provides personalized links based on your profile and the information you have provided.

The Resource Center is an organized catalog of relevant services, resources, wellness, and financial tools to support student-veteran success. It connects users to relevant academic and career services, wellness, financial, and personal development tools to support their academic success "to, through, and beyond" higher education. SVA is committed to fostering a community where veterans may thrive by offering a range of services tailored to veterans' unique needs. Navigating life after serving can be a challenging experience. Here, student veterans, dependents, and caregivers may find a welcoming network filled with camaraderie and expert support.

Academic Services and Support: Service to School has partnered with select educational institutions to form VetLink, a network of schools dedicated to expanding access and opportunity for student veterans.

Warrior-Scholar Project: This project hosts intense, one—and two-week college preparatory academic "boot camps" for enlisted veterans and transitioning service members.

Career Development: FourBlock is a nationwide community of veterans and employers dedicated to easing the transition process for veterans. It aims to equip veterans to secure jobs and pursue careers that align with their calling. Career One-Stop provides integrated, easy-to-understand workforce information that helps job seekers, students, workers, workforce intermediaries, and employers develop their skills and make informed economic decisions in the new economy. Access FourBlock via the Career Center.

LinkedIn offers free resources and training on maximizing and leveraging LinkedIn for military and veteran job seekers. Service members, veterans, military spouses, Fry Scholars, and VA Caregivers may receive a free one-year LinkedIn Premium (Job Seeker) membership.

The My Career Advancement Account Scholarship is a workforce development program that provides up to $4,000 of tuition assistance to eligible military spouses.

Veterati is a free mentorship platform that connects service members, veterans, and military spouses with unlimited mentors.

The Military Spouse Advocacy Network connects military spouses to the resources they need from the very beginning.

The career center provides services to ensure career readiness, including workshops, hiring fairs, and networking events. You may connect in the SVA Career Nexus to explore curated opportunities from premium employers dedicated to hiring our nation's best talent.

The SVA Job Board lets you connect with employers who value your military service and embark on a journey to achieve your career aspirations through the camaraderie of an excited and supportive community. More partners will be joining the job board soon. You may also look up the corporations, foundations, and nonprofit organizations with which SVA partners.

The VMock is an online resume review tool that leverages technologies such as data science, machine learning, and natural language processing to provide instant, personalized feedback on resumes.

FourBlock's Career Readiness Program helps transitioning veterans develop a relationship-based career strategy. Veterans connect with new companies each week to hear career advice, discover new industries, and begin building the right network for meaningful careers. Find more information at https://studentveterans.org/success-hub/career-center/.

SVA- APEX

Access APEX - SVA's Academic+Career Pathway Explorer. APEX is more than a career exploration platform. It's an intricate tool designed to align your distinct experiences, interests, and aspirations as a student veteran with tangible career opportunities, academic programs, colleges and universities, or certifications and licenses that can prepare you for your dream career.

APEX allows you to: self-assess prior experiences and education to reveal occupations and career pathways aligned to your skills and interests; view and apply to current job opportunities from SVA partner employers; understand academic programs, certifications, and training that can prepare you for your desired career.

APEX can assist in finding your best-fit college or university with veteran-relevant data to help you make an informed decision about where to use your earned veteran education benefits. Explore skill-building activities that allow you to network at your college or within your local community to help you prepare to enter your ideal career. Discover your favorite degree programs, schools, occupations, and career pathways for easy comparison later.

APEX enables you to organize and complete action items assigned by your Success Coach during coaching sessions, keeping you on track. You may also find inspiring success stories from mentors and other student veterans like you.

While APEX can help you explore and find your new path alone, SVA success coaches can help you navigate your next steps, using the information you enter in your MySVA profile and APEX to help you decide about your future and how to get there. Request a coaching session on the Success Coaching tab in MySVA for more guided assistance with creating a map for success.

SVA- Programs

SVA conducts various events annually. The National Conference (NatCon) occurs every January. Washington Week is typically held in late February or early March, depending on the Senate Committee's Hearing schedule. The Leadership Institute is held in Washington, D.C., in the fall. Regional Summits take place during the summer. Locations vary every year. Find more information about these programs at https://studentveterans.org/programs-events/.

SVA NatCon is the largest gathering of student veterans worldwide. SVA has chapters at nearly 1,600 U.S. campuses and several countries abroad. NatCon is a focal point in the academic year for sharing ideas and best practices, as well as networking with veteran and military-affiliated students, their families and caregivers, supporters, allies, corporate, government, and nonprofit partners, and more.

Visit https://studentveterans.org/programs-events/national-conference/ for more information on NatCon.

Regional summits are often referred to as Mini-NatCons. They provide tools, techniques, and tactics needed for student veterans to run a successful and sustainable student organization. Regional summits are definitive experiences for planning and building a successful SVA chapter. They are recommended for all current/future chapter leaders, chapter members, and university faculty, staff, and administration involved in the chapter.

Networking opportunities combined with the lessons delivered will help SVA chapters become successful and sustainable for those who come after us. Find information on the regional summit in your area at https://studentveterans.org/programs-events/regional-summits/.

The Leadership Institute is an immersive program that prepares students to effect change beyond their SVA chapter and campus. This premier student leadership experience brings together our country's top chapter leaders to equip tomorrow's leaders to serve and create a lasting community of impact. The Leadership Institute is open to all chapter leaders who are currently enrolled or have recently graduated. Virtual Leadership Institute attendees are welcome to apply for this year's event.

The application process is competitive. If selected, Student Veterans of America will cover the cost of your travel to Washington, D.C., to develop your core values and hone your leadership skills. You will return to campus with the tools needed to serve others more effectively, a lasting network to support you, and an expectation to expand your impact on your campus, community, and country. Learn more information about the Leadership Institute at
https://studentveterans.org/programs-events/leadership-institute/.

SVA- Advocacy

Washington Week is SVA's premier advocacy and legislative event. SVA's policy and advocacy priorities are formally published each March through events around Capitol Hill, the White House, and the various Executive Branch departments and agencies. Washington Week allows SVA members to make their voices heard in the heart of our nation's capital. Chapter

members have the opportunity to share their experience as student veterans with their elected officials, participate with SVA and other VSOs as they present their policy priorities to Congress, network, and experience the rich history of Washington, D.C. Read more about Washington Week at
https://studentveterans.org/programs-events/washington-week/.

SVA works closely with Congress and the federal government to promote forward-looking policies to help veterans get the education they need to thrive in the modern workforce. Its work focuses on myriad issues, and they prepare analyses of various proposals concerning matters affecting veterans in higher education. As subject matter experts on higher education and veteran policy, Congress and senior government officials frequently call on SVA's team to deliver testimony regarding topics facing student veterans. The primary focus is on student-veterans' success, and the SVA achieves a high level of influence through consistent liaison with Congress, relevant organizations and associations, industry, and others concerned with proposed and pending policies.

The SVA team has testified on the Transition Assistance Program (TAP), student debt, and the Veteran Success on Campus program (VSOC). SVA has advised the administration on the GI Bill Comparison Tool, intergovernmental policy, such as the agreement with the Federal Trade Commission, and numerous proposals affecting the Post-9/11 GI Bill.

SVA constantly informs and advocates for new legislation that may positively affect a student veteran's quality of life while keeping the community informed about legal/regulatory changes.

SVA's work includes advocating for policy and legislative improvements that enhance topics such as the investment and impact of the GI Bill, STEM education pathways, in-state tuition, student debt, accessibility, priority enrollment for student veterans, and compliance, credits, and credentialing. Find details on legislation and policy goals at
https://studentveterans.org/government-affairs/.

SVA- Community Service

SVA partners with community and non-profit organizations within the local community and at our major events. Its partners include the American Red Cross, the Mission Continues, Adopt-A-Highway, and projects with local and state Parks and Recreation agencies. SVA has participated in joint service projects with various VSOs, such as the VFW and the Legion, both nationally and at the local chapter level. SVA also supports events sponsored by the VA to help veterans, their dependents, and caregivers. Local SVA chapters support and participate in community service activities to the extent a chapter is available to do so. Engaging in community service activities also fulfills a social aspect of belonging.

American Legion (Legion)

The Legion is one of the largest VSOs. Established in 1919, it advocates for the needs of every generation of veterans, service members, and their families who pledge to protect our nation. Today, the Legion is committed to destigmatizing mental health support, offering peer-to-peer resources, and empowering everyone to "Be the One" in the fight to prevent veteran suicide.

The Legion provides veterans with access to their VA benefits and has service officers to assist with navigating the VA enrollment and accessibility system. Accredited Legion service officers offer free assistance to veterans and their families with VA disability benefits applications and VA education and employment services. These services are available through the local Legion Hall or the Community Veterans Service Office.

The Legion also has auxiliary units- such as the American Legion Auxiliary, the Sons of the American Legion, and the Legion Riders- that address the family element of veteran life and contribute to community service. Legion Riders are known for fundraising for local children's hospitals, schools, veterans' homes, severely wounded servicemembers, and scholarships. Find information about the Legion at https://www.legion.org/.

Legion- Advocacy

The Be the One initiative aims to reduce the veteran suicide rate. The Legion actively works to lessen the stigma associated with mental health treatment and empower everyone to take appropriate action when a veteran or service member may be at risk, one life at a time. Find more information on this and other advocacy areas at https://www.legion.org/advocacy. These issues include grassroots, education, flag advocacy, voting, and youth support.

The Legion advocates for issues, including the Major Richard Star Act, which would not allow disability payments to be deducted from one's retirement pay. The Legion advocates for survivors to be able to keep their benefits without penalty for remarrying before age 55. Currently, benefits are lost if the survivor remarries before the age of 55. Information may be found at https://www.votervoice.net/AmericanLegion/home.

The Legislative Division promotes the Legion's position and recommendations to Congress. Services include lobbying members of Congress, efficiently communicating issues and concerns with those on the Hill, and education and awareness about various issues and concerns affecting veterans. Find more information at https://www.legion.org/advocacy/legislative/about-the-national-legislative-division.

Legion- Community Service

The American Legion has a proud tradition of supporting our nation's youth. It was founded on this principle in 1919, when Children & Youth was declared one of the Legion's four pillars. Since then, several youth-oriented programs have been developed, including Temporary Financial Assistance, Family Support Network, and child safety and well-being programs.

The Americanism Commission's Children & Youth Committee is the center of the Legion's youth-support efforts. The committee meets annually to formulate, recommend and implement plans, programs and activities designed to: assure care and protection for children of veterans; improve conditions for all children and youth with due concern for maintaining the integrity of the family home; prevent social and physical ills of children and youth where possible, utilizing services of and cooperating with sound organizations and agencies for children and youth; maintain a balanced program that provides for their physical, emotional, intellectual and spiritual needs.

The American Legion has always strongly advocated for children and youth. This steadfast dedication continues to be a driving force on behalf of children across the country. More information is available at https://www.legion.org/advocacy/youth-support.

The Legion provides youth and family support resources, including community education, substance abuse prevention, victim services, youth organizations, and youth programs. Learn more at https://www.legion.org/advocacy/youth-support/youth-support-resources.

Veterans of Foreign Wars (VFW)

The VFW is a non-profit organization founded in 1899 to foster camaraderie among U.S. veterans of overseas conflicts, to serve veterans, the military, and our communities, and to advocate for all veterans. The VFW's vision is to ensure veterans are respected for their service, always receive their earned entitlement, and are recognized for the sacrifices they and their loved ones have made for this great country.

Founded in 1914, the VFW Auxiliary is a separate organization within the VFW Post, serving as the backbone of many local VFW and community service projects. The Auxiliary supports its host Post and comprises veterans' dependents and family members. It is as active and influential on the Hill as the VFW proper. Find information about the VFW at https://www.vfw.org/.

VFW- Advocacy

VFW is among the most respected voices in Washington, D.C., and within local governments across America. It advocates for justice for our nation's veterans, service members, and military families on various issues and continues to be the voice for veterans everywhere. VFW regularly testifies before Congress, meets with elected officials, and rallies its national network of members and supporters to ensure our lawmakers put veterans first. When those who have served their country and those who support them stand together, the VFW cannot be ignored.

The VFW holds an annual VFW Washington Conference, which equates to the SVA's Washington Week. This week, the VFW and other VSOs will give veterans a voice on the Hill regarding VA benefits and policies, including the 2024 Senator Elizabeth Dole 21st Century Veterans Healthcare and Benefits Improvement Act and the Not Just a Number Act.

The local Post is the foundation for all VFW activities. Posts are organized into districts in each state. Hierarchy includes Post officers, District officers, and State officers. The next level is national officers.
Further information may be found at
https://www.vfw.org/advocacy.

VFW- Community Service

In 2024, VFW provided $30,000 for flood victims in Iowa, $10,000 for victims of Hurricane Helene in Tennessee, $100,000 for victims of Hurricane Helene in North Carolina, $20,000 for victims of Hurricane Helene in Georgia, and $673,000 to Posts and VFW Auxiliary for community service grants.

VFW- Programs

Department Service Officers (DSOs): A global network of highly trained and accredited service officers helps veterans navigate the complex VA claims process. Department of Veterans Affairs statistics show that in 2024, VFW helped recoup $14.6 billion in earned benefits on behalf of approximately 146,000 veterans. VFW's Pre-Discharge claims representatives also filed 14,000 VA claims, resulting in more than $110 million in disability compensation for transitioning service members. The VFW offers this service at no charge.

Pre-Discharge Program: Introduced in 2001, VFW's pre-discharge program (formerly known as Benefits Delivery at Discharge) provides claims assistance to separating military personnel on more than 20 military installations and military-populated regions throughout the nation, including the military district of the Washington, D.C. area. Read more about VFW programs at https://www.vfw.org/about-us.

Wounded Warrior Project (WWP)

Every veteran eventually has a journey to transition to civilian life. That journey looks different for wounded warriors, their families, and caregivers. WWP began in 2003 as an effort to provide simple care and comfort items to the hospital bedsides of the first wounded service members returning home from the conflicts in Iraq and Afghanistan. As our veterans' needs have evolved, so have the services of WWP. Today, through their direct programs in mental health, career counseling, long-term rehabilitative care, and advocacy efforts, the WWP improves the lives of millions of veterans, their families, and caregivers.

Learn more at
https://www.woundedwarriorproject.org/.

WWP- Advocacy

WWP uses warriors' feedback and insights to inform those on the Hill of veterans' issues and concerns. The WWP advocates for veteran policies and initiatives that make a tangible difference, enhancing the lives of millions of veterans, their family members, and caregivers.

WWP's legislative priorities for 2024 were mental health and suicide prevention, brain health and TBI, women veterans, economic empowerment, transition support, toxic exposure, and severely wounded service members and veterans.

Find more information at https://www.woundedwarriorproject.org/programs/government-affairs.

WWP- Community Service

WWP believes no one organization can alone meet the needs of all wounded, injured, or ill veterans. By collaborating with other military and veteran support organizations, we amplify the effects of our efforts. Our investments and unfunded partnerships in the military and veteran community fill gaps in our programs and reinforce our existing efforts.

Since 2012, WWP has committed almost $388 million to 215 military and veteran organizations. In addition to $200 million in direct programs and services in 2024, WWP has provided grants to 43 organizations that support and serve our nation's veterans and their families.

Alongside our co-chairs at the Elizabeth Dole Foundation, WWP leads the Hidden Helpers Coalition (HHC), a collective of more than 108 nonprofits, corporations, and government entities dedicated to supporting caregivers of children and youth. WWP continues to invest in organizations that drive innovative, tailored solutions that connect and empower the youngest caregivers of our nation's wounded warriors. The organizations include the Cohen Veterans Network, the Comfort Crew, Our Military Kids, the National Military Family Association, the Military Child Education Coalition, and others. Learn more at https://www.woundedwarriorproject.org/programs/community-partners.

Disabled American Veterans (DAV)

DAV helps more than a million veterans every year. It helps veterans find assistance with VA benefits, medical transportation, employment, entrepreneurship, and transition services.

Benefits and policies for veterans continue to change and become more complex from year to year. The system can be hard to navigate. It takes knowledge and persistence to understand what is available, what is required to file the right claims, how to manage appeals, and most importantly, how to see the process through.

DAV's professional benefits advocates are available throughout the U.S. and Puerto Rico and can help. They're at VA hospitals, DAV locations, and installations, and are ready to counsel service members on claims, whether they separate or even many years later. Last year, 561,358 claims were presented to the Veterans Benefits Administration under DAV representation for 1,538,112 specific injuries and illnesses, and DAV-represented claimants received more than $30.4 billion in benefits. For more information, please visit https://www.dav.org/.

DAV- Advocacy

DAV communicates its legislative priorities to Congress, the media, and the general public. Given the volatility of the current political environment, strengthening advocacy efforts is essential so that the much-talked-about reform of VA's health care system is done in the best interest of veterans, with existing benefits protected and future benefits developed in line with what matters to those who have served.

The 2025 Critical Policy Goals include strengthening policies to ensure that toxic-exposed veterans receive earned benefits promptly, eliminate gaps in mental health care and suicide prevention, to prevent Congress or the VA from reducing, offsetting, or taxing veterans benefits, to modernize and strengthen benefits for survivors, expand comprehensive dental care services to all service-disabled veterans, to enhance long-term care by providing assisted-living, increasing caregiver support, and to sustain the VA health care system by reforming infrastructure planning and funding mechanisms. Learn more information at https://www.dav.org/get-involved/advocate-on-legislation/.

DAV- Community Service

DAV helps veterans and their families in life-changing ways. In-person support on military bases across the country helps veterans transition to accessing benefits and successfully reintegrate into civilian life. Additionally, DAV hosts job fairs online and nationwide, connecting veterans with employers, tools, resources, and opportunities. With a national/local support network, including over 1,200 chapters and nearly 100 offices nationwide. DAV volunteers offer support on-site at many VA medical centers, providing more than a million volunteer hours annually. DAV also provides no-cost rides to and from VA medical appointments and offers emergency grants to ill and injured veterans living in areas affected by natural disasters. DAV also connects homeless and at-risk veterans with care, benefits, and employment opportunities.

Iraq & Afghanistan Veterans of America (IAVA)

The IAVA increases awareness in the media, among the American public, and in Washington, D.C., to ensure the voices of our newest generation of veterans are heard and listened to. The IAVA fights on behalf of the post-9/11 generation of veterans. Learn more information at https://iava.org/.

IAVA- Advocacy

IAVA fights and wins battles for the post-9/11 generation of veterans. Members tell IAVA what is essential and engage policymakers and the media to bring positive change. IAVA is the voice of Iraq and Afghanistan veterans that they may rely on to advance their collective goals in Washington. IAVA's nonpartisan advocacy work ensures post-9/11 veterans and their families are supported, protected, and never forgotten.

American veterans remain deeply troubled by the chaotic exit by the U.S. from Afghanistan in the summer of 2021. Nearly all the Afghans who partnered with us during the war were left behind.

The IAVA advocates for passing into law a means to ensure our Afghan allies gain the legal status in the U.S. they were promised. IAVA supports urging your senator to vote 'yes' on a critical National Security Act 2024 amendment, which supports our Afghan allies.

IAVA advocates to empower veterans wishing to use medical cannabis. 88% of IAVA members surveyed support the additional research of medical cannabis to help them face war injuries such as PTSD and TBI. IAVA is dedicated to fostering a national conversation on the need for bipartisan, data-based solutions that can relieve millions.

IAVA needs veterans to urge Congress and the current administration to enact the bipartisan VA Medicinal Cannabis Research Act (S. 326/ H.R. 1003) so the VA may conduct research into the efficacy of medical cannabis as a treatment for veterans with chronic pain, PTSD, and other conditions. Find more information at https://iava.org/advocacy.

Paralyzed Veterans of America (PVA)

Paralyzed Veterans of America is the only nonprofit Veteran Service Organization dedicated solely to helping Veterans with spinal cord injuries and disorders (SCI/D), and diseases, like MS and ALS.

With charitable contributions and donations, PVA has helped millions of Veterans, their family members, caregivers, and those living with SCI/D. To date, PVA has raised over $1.2 billion, secured for the veterans and families it represents.

In 2022 alone, PVA has raised over $32.8 million for veterans' accessible home remodeling, over $9.6 million to make veterans' cars wheelchair-accessible, and over $1.1 million for research to find treatments and a cure for paralysis.

PVA's mission is to ensure every veteran of every age, every branch, and every conflict regains what they fought for: their freedom and independence. For more information, please visit https://pva.org/.

PVA- Advocacy

For nearly 80 years, PVA has led the fight for accessibility and provided a full circle of support from injury or diagnosis to life's milestones.

To help disabled veterans lead independent, healthy, and productive lives, PVA focuses on the whole veteran: physical health, financial security, societal needs, and mental well-being. PVA maintains offices inside every VA SCI/D center across the U.S. Staffed with licensed architects, medical professionals, legal experts, and leaders in research and education, PVA fights to help veterans with SCI/D receive the benefits they earned, the specialized health care they deserve, the accessible homes and vehicles they need, and the meaningful careers they want. PVA also advocates for disabled veterans with the most significant support needs to have access to the same opportunities and freedoms available to all Americans.

Some acts that the PVA advocates for include the Driver Reimbursement Increase for Veteran Equality Act, the Veterans Accessibility Advisory Committee Act, and the Credit for Caring Act, as well as protecting the VA SCI/D system of care. More information is available at https://pva.org/research-resources/policy-priorities/.

PVA- Community Service

The PVA offers Caregiver Support, assistance in finding a national service officer, legal support, medical services, a connection with the VA for benefits, the Veterans Career Program, adaptive sports, and other veteran resources.

Caregiver resources listed include the VA Caregiver Support Line (1-855-260-3274), links for VA Caregiver Support, the VA Caregiver Toolbox, Hidden Heroes (resources for military caregivers), and the Elizabeth Dole Foundation. Access more information at https://pva.org/find-support/caregiver-support/.

Academic Organizations

Admissions/Enrollment. This office assists students in completing the necessary paperwork, processing their applications, and providing the required documentation.

Financial Aid. This office assists students in applying for grants, loans, and scholarships. It maintains students' financial records of payments and credits, aid applied for and received, tuition and fees, meals, lodging, and other academic-related expenses on campus. VA education benefits are applied here if not part of the enrollment process.

Academic Advisor/Counselor. Each student should be assigned an individual to guide their degree plan, class selection, course schedule, and other academic concerns involving degree or career planning.

Academic Affairs. This office handles all academic issues and concerns, including problems with instructors, curriculum, certification, grades, and syllabi.

Student Affairs. This office handles all issues and concerns within student organizations, as well as student issues and concerns that are not classroom-related but related to academic life. Student services often fall into this category.

Academic- Veteran Service Organizations/ Veteran Student Organizations on Campus

Organizations or offices focused on serving the student-veteran have many labels. For example, the student-veteran support agency at the University of Alabama is the Office of Veterans and Military Affairs. Other labels include the Student-Veteran Resource Center at the University of Georgia, the Military and Veteran Services (MVS) at NC State University, Military Outreach at Georgia State University, and the Office of Veterans Affairs and Services at Penn State (Burke, 2022a, 2022b). The Military and Veteran Affiliated Division supports Austin Peay State University student veterans.

Whatever the label, the mission is essentially the same: to facilitate the success of student-veterans. These offices offer numerous services to accomplish this mission, including assistance with enrollment and filing for VA education benefits.

The best veteran service facilities on campus have personnel certified by the VA in their respective areas of responsibility (VA education benefits, VA job placement and training, VA health, VA disability, etc.). The on-campus veteran service facility should be a one-stop shop for all the needs of student veterans, their dependents, and caregivers, from entering the institution to their academic life and experience.

Non-Academic

Numerous organizations and agencies, neither government nor academic, also meet the needs of transitioning veterans. The agencies and organizations presented do not represent all the resources available.

Hire Heroes USA

Hire Heroes USA is one of the country's most effective nonprofit organizations focused on veteran employment. Its impact is demonstrated in its results: over 1,000,000 confirmed hires, 36,000+ jobs posted on its job board, and 1,450+ volunteers.

Hire Heroes USA helps U.S. servicemembers and their spouses achieve success at home through rewarding career paths. After all they have given our nation, we want to help them find the support they need to make their next steps successful. Hire Heroes USA relies on donations to complete its mission.

Hire Heroes USA provides free job search assistance to U.S. military members, veterans, and spouses, and helps companies connect with opportunities to hire them. Whether looking for full-time, part-time, or remote work, Hire Heroes USA will help you meet your employment goals. Services are personalized to you and are available to U.S. military members, veterans, and military spouses free of charge.

Companies may become involved in veteran transition. Whether companies want to hire veterans or support their transition, there are several ways your company can connect with Hire Heroes USA's mission and make a difference. More information may be found at https://www.hireheroesusa.org/.

Fisher House Foundation

The Fisher House Foundation builds comfort homes where military and veteran families may stay free of charge while a loved one is in the hospital. These homes are located at military and VA medical centers around the world. Fisher Houses have up to 21 suites, each featuring a private bedroom and bath. Families share a common kitchen, laundry facilities, a warm dining room, and an inviting living room.

Since its inception, the program has saved military and veterans' families an estimated $610 million in out-of-pocket costs for lodging and transportation. The Fisher House Foundation also operates the Hero Miles program, utilizing donated frequent-flyer miles to transport family members to the bedside of injured service members, and the Hotels for Heroes program, which utilizes donated hotel points to provide complimentary accommodations for family members at hotels near medical centers. The Foundation also manages a grant program that supports other charitable organizations and scholarship funds for military children, spouses, and the children of fallen and disabled veterans.

For more than 30 years, the Fisher House program has provided a home away from home for families of patients receiving medical care at major military and VA medical centers. These homes offer free, temporary lodging to military and veteran families, allowing them to be close to their loved one during a medical crisis and focus on what is important—the healing process. As of November 2024, there are 99 Fisher Houses located in the United States, Germany, and the United Kingdom.

Fisher House facilities have a daily capacity of 1,400 families, having served more than 534,000 since its inception in 1990. The cumulative number of lodging days offered is over 12.5 million. Fifteen thousand students have received $ 29 million in scholarship awards. Hero Miles provided more than 70,000 airline tickets to service members and their families, worth nearly $124 million. Learn more information at https://fisherhouse.org/.

Elizabeth Dole Foundation (EDF)

Caregivers play an essential role in many veterans' transitions. The Elizabeth Dole Foundation (EDF) provides support to caregivers, veterans, and service organizations, helping them advocate in Congress to address the unique needs and challenges caregivers face.

Established in 2012, the foundation empowers military and veteran caregivers, as well as their families and communities, through various programs, partnerships, and advocacy efforts. These initiatives aim to foster innovation and sustainable solutions, exemplified by the Elizabeth Dole Home Care Act of 2023.

Some 290 caregiver fellows nationwide provide a voice in Congress and resources on the ground.

Programs the foundation supports include the Hidden Heroes Campaign, a public awareness campaign bringing vital attention to the untold stories of military and veteran caregivers, seeking solutions for the tremendous challenges and long-term needs they face.

The Hidden Helper's Coalition is a national alliance comprising public and private sector organizations that aim to amplify the voices of military and veteran caregiver children, teens, and young adults, and to enhance the services and support available to them.

The Campaign for Inclusive Care is a strategic joint initiative between EDF and the VA to transform the culture of care at the VA, making it fully inclusive of caregivers from the onset of the care journey.

Founded by the USAA, Face the Fight is a collaborative effort of corporations, foundations, nonprofits, and veteran-focused organizations charged with raising awareness and support for veteran suicide prevention. Their mission is to break the stigmas surrounding suicide to open conversation and offer support around the topic. Facing the reality of veteran suicide is a struggle. Face the Fight believes when people face this fight together, there is hope. More information on suicide-prevention resources and assistance is available at https://wefacethefight.org/#join-the-fight.

Launched in 2023, Mental Wellness at EDF offers military and veteran caregivers a safe, supportive virtual space to connect with peers via structured workshops and themed care groups organized around shared life experiences. The Caregiver Mental Wellness Workshop is a six-week virtual program designed for military and veteran caregivers to come together in a safe, structured space to reflect on their mental wellness experiences as they relate to their role as caregivers. Participants receive and provide support to peers, identify and improve coping strategies, discover available resources, and learn how to establish and practice self-care.

Join or support the foundation in helping America's caregivers, their families, and their communities thrive at https://www.elizabethdolefoundation.org/.

National Veterans Foundation (NVF)

The National Veterans Foundation's mission is to serve the crisis management, information, and referral needs of all U.S. veterans and their families through the management and operation of the nation's oldest toll-free, vet-to-vet helpline for all veterans and their families. Public awareness programs consistently spotlight the needs of America's veterans. Outreach services provide veterans and their families in need with food, clothing, transportation, employment assistance, and other essential resources.

The National Veterans Foundation's Lifeline for Vets helps veterans of all eras, their family members, and active-duty service members, including some who are serving overseas in combat deployments. The Lifeline for Vets assists veterans with needs including medical treatment, PTSD counseling, VA benefits advocacy, food, shelter, employment, training, legal aid, suicide intervention, and more.

The need for the National Veterans Foundation's services has never been greater. More than 2.5 million Americans have served in the wars in Iraq and Afghanistan. Estimates are that one out of every five Iraq and Afghanistan Veterans suffers from TBI, PTSD, or major depression. About 7% of Iraq and Afghanistan Veterans are unemployed. An estimated 50,000 Veterans are homeless on any given night. Twenty-two veterans a day, men and women, commit suicide.

The Lifeline for Vets provides a unique and much-needed service for these veterans. Because it is non-governmental, it provides a proven Vet-to-Vet service model. It provides veterans with a referral source that offers local and national, situation-appropriate solutions for their various problems.

Lifeline for Vets counselors have access to one of the most comprehensive databases of local, national, community-based, and government resources at their fingertips. Veterans can call Lifeline for Vets to receive help with financial problems, mental health issues, accessing their VA benefits and healthcare, employment, housing, family counseling, and many other issues.

Lifeline for Vets counselors aim to provide appropriate solutions for veterans calling the hotline. It might be as simple as finding the closest VA facility, or as complicated as connecting them with local resources to assist with a financial, legal, or medical/psychological problem. Counselors endeavor to follow up with every veteran who calls the hotline to determine if the solution is effective or if additional resources are needed. For example, a veteran who calls for assistance at a VA facility may find that they need help with transportation after the initial call or assistance from a counselor in completing VA paperwork.

More information may be found at https://nvf.org/.

United Service Organization (USO)

From the moment they enlist, through assignments and deployments, and as they transition back to their communities, today's military can rely on the USO because of donations from supporters. Most noted for their entertainment shows for troops deployed overseas, USO goes where other non-profit organizations cannot reach to make service members feel supported and understood.

Since 1941, USO has been the nation's leading organization serving the men and women in the U.S. military and their families throughout their time in uniform. From enlistment through transition back to their communities, the USO is always by their side.

Today's USO continuously adapts to the needs of our men and women in uniform and their families so they can focus on their critical mission. USO centers operate at or near military installations across the United States and worldwide, including in combat zones and even unstaffed USO service sites in places too dangerous for anyone but combat troops to occupy.

USO airport centers nationwide offer around-the-clock hospitality for traveling service members and their families. USO tours bring America and its celebrities to service members assigned far from home to entertain and convey the nation's support. Many specialized programs offer a continuum of support to service members throughout their service journey, from the first time they don the uniform until the last time they take it off.

USO programs do more than keep service members and families connected; they also work to strengthen wellness and resiliency. Coffee Connection Live with Brittany Boccher was established to create a safe space for military spouses to connect with one another while learning valuable tools to help in their everyday lives. This social-connection program also assists transitioning service members.

On average, military spouses move up to 12 times during a 20-year military career, often needing to start over each time. They also deal with the struggles associated with meeting new people and establishing a sense of connectedness within their new home and community.

In 2016, USO launched a worldwide initiative to strengthen and empower military spouses by connecting them to others in their communities, simply over coffee, an activity, or a community outing. These gatherings allow spouses to relax comfortably, share advice, learn about local attractions, and make new friends in a relaxed and casual atmosphere. Spouses are encouraged to bring other military spouses to join in on the friendly conversation.

Each Coffee Connections location customizes events. USO statistics indicate that service members and military families participated in over 12,000 Coffee Connections events in 2024 alone.

Continuing Your Journey monthly workshops cover topics from self-reflection to DIY decluttering and vision boards. In these one-hour workshops, Brittany and a special guest provide military spouses with the tips, tools, and resources necessary to prioritize self-care and personal development. These workshops aim to help pinpoint and focus on specific areas for improvement.

Discovering Your Spark is a series of quarterly, two-and-a-half-hour workshops that enable military spouses to discover their passion and purpose, approaching life's challenges with a more positive outlook. These workshops help spouses focus on discovering their purpose.

The USO understands the strong bond between humans and animals- and the critical roles dogs can play within the military community in addressing mental, emotional, and physical needs. The USO Canine Program includes therapy dogs, family pets, and military working dog programs. Interacting with therapy dogs may reduce stress and provide a unique morale boost for service members and their families. Including canine family members in programs enables families to participate more fully in USO activities and feel a sense of connection to their community. USO's support of military working dogs honors their contribution and that of their human handlers, who also feel cared for as their canine battle buddy is acknowledged.

USO is proud to offer the USO Reading Program. In the spirit of bringing military families together, the program is primarily driven by virtual, on-demand story time offerings that help the USO extend its reach. The program was utilized 47,000 times by service members and their families in 2024. The USO Reading Program enables service members to read to their children from anywhere in the world. When a service member stationed in the deserts of Kuwait misses the birth of their child, the USO is there to provide that powerful connection back home. Through the USO Reading Program, service members may read bedtime stories to a newborn child from halfway around the globe. They may walk into a participating USO location, record themselves reading their child's favorite story, and have that recording shipped home.

USO Special Delivery combines baby shower games, local guest speakers, drawings for traditional baby shower gifts, and creating community connections. These popular showers provide a touch of home for parents-to-be, who are often away from their families, friends, and support networks during pregnancy and within the first few months of infancy. USO Special Delivery is also offered virtually, with video-call baby showers that reach remote military communities located far from a USO center, where a traditional, in-person baby shower might not be possible. More than 5,000 service members and military families participated in the USO Special Delivery Program in 2024. In fact, close to 75% of all attendees worldwide that year told USO Special Delivery Program staff that it was the only shower they'd receive to help them celebrate the arrival of their new family member. Information on these and additional USO programs is available at https://www.uso.org/programs.

USO is not part of the federal government. A private organization powered by volunteers, USO relies on the generosity of individuals, organizations, and corporations to support its activities and accomplish its mission of connection. Learn more at https://www.uso.org/.

Tragedy Assistance Program for Veterans Survivors (TAPS)

Since 1994, TAPS has provided a variety of no-cost programs to survivors nationally and worldwide, offering comfort and hope to families and loved ones-through a 24/7 peer-support network and connection to grief resources. TAPS' National Military Survivor Seminar and Good Grief Camp have been held annually in Washington, D.C., over Memorial Day weekend. TAPS also conducts regional survivor seminars for adult and youth programs at locations nationwide, as well as retreats and expeditions worldwide. Staff can connect you to counseling in your community and help you navigate benefits and resources.

TAPS offers several programs and resources, including a survivor helpline, a survivor care team, grief counselors, case work, educational assistance, a caregiver-to-survivor program, survivor advocacy, the TAPS Institute, TAPS magazines and publications, survivor connections, and others. More information may be found at https://www.taps.org/resources/.

TAPS programs offer a place of companionship. Every TAPS program is designed to help survivors feel comforted as they grieve, supported as they rebuild, and united with other survivors as they choose to hope. Seminars or online gatherings offer practical advice, sharing groups, and opportunities to connect with others who are facing similar challenges. Young survivors grieve together, play together, and learn to laugh again at Good Grief Camp. Local communities support other survivors at care groups or TAPS Together activities. Adults find opportunities to create healthy habits, seek hope, and connect with nature at Women's Empowerment and Men's Programming events. Moreover, survivors rediscover traditions and memories through our sports and entertainment events.

Through various programs, TAPS helps survivors create rich lives despite loss. TAPS seminars are inclusive, discussion-based events that include workshops for understanding and processing grief, as well as small-group sharing sessions where survivors can connect with peers.

TAPS online groups and workshops are available wherever survivors are in the grief cycle- and wherever they are in the world. They facilitate easy and meaningful connections among survivors. Peer mentors- survivors 18 months past their loss- guide fellow survivors who have experienced a similar loss and are looking for support from someone who truly understands.

TAPS enables survivors to find local support, such as a local military family survivor support group, and enables them to meet with people who understand what they're going through for emotional support and camaraderie.

TAPS offers various family-oriented programs. The Women's Empowerment program connects grieving women with other survivors to offer comfort and support during their grief. This vibrant, compassionate community is a place of support and inspiration. The Men's program acknowledges that most men need other men to pave the way for them to grieve. Join other surviving men to lean on each other and share experiences, strength, and hope. The Young Adults program is for 18- to 30-year-old military survivors, focusing on the 5 Pillars of growth and healing during the grief journey.

TAPS provides compassionate care to all survivors of military suicide loss, to help stabilize survivors and family members, leading them toward healing and growth.

TAPS Togethers are one-day, organized, social events across the country, led by TAPS staff or survivors like you, to expand TAPS' ever-growing peer-support community.

Team TAPS honors fallen heroes through running, walking, biking, and other events. You can participate in an organized Team TAPS event nationwide or host your own.

TAPS also organizes sports and entertainment programs. Stars4TAPS and Teams4TAPS connect surviving military families with professional sports programs and the entertainment industry to bring hope and healing while honoring their fallen heroes. More information about TAPS programs may be found at https://www.taps.org/programs/.

If you are grieving the loss of a fallen service member or know someone who could use TAPS support, the toll-free TAPS 24/7 National Military Survivor Helpline is available toll-free, offering loving support and resources at 800-959-TAPS (8277). More information may be found at https://www.taps.org/.

Operation Home Front

Operation Homefront, a nationally recognized 501(c)(3) nonprofit organization, builds strong, stable, and secure military families so they may thrive, not simply struggle to get by, in the communities they have worked so hard to protect. Since 2002, Operation Homefront has proudly served America's military families, providing relief and recurring family support programs and services year-round to help military families overcome short-term difficulties, so they do not become long-term hardships.

Leading independent charity oversight groups recognized Operation Homefront for superior performance. Eighty-three percent of its expenditure is allocated directly to programs that support thousands of military families annually.

By connecting the American donor community to military families through a robust array of valued and life-changing programs that address specific short-term and critical financial needs, long-term stability, and recurring support requirements, Operation Homefront helps military families overcome many challenges inherent in military life. The results are stronger, more stable, and more secure military families. Programs include short-term assistance and relief programs, as well as recurring family support programs.

Short-term programs include the Critical Financial Assistance Program, Transitional Housing (villages), Transitional Housing (apartments), Transitional Homes for Veterans, and Permanent Homes for Veterans.

Recurring family support programs include the Back-to-School Brigade, Holiday Meals for Military, Star-Spangled Babies, Holiday Toy Drive, Homefront Celebrations, and Military Child of the Year. Learn more information at https://operationhomefront.org/about-us/.

Operation Homefront has provided over 210,000 holiday meals to military and veteran families. Over 720 families are housed in permanent homes for veterans, surpassing $104 million in needed home equity for military families. More than $44 million in relief has been given through the Critical Financial Assistance Program, with over 57,000 requests fulfilled. Nearly 600,000 backpacks with school supplies have been distributed to military children.

For more information on Operation Homefront and how to support or join their mission, please visit https://operationhomefront.org/.

Vet Dogs

The service dog programs of America's VetDogs were created to provide enhanced mobility and renewed independence to veterans, active-duty service members, and first responders with disabilities, enabling them to live with pride and self-reliance once again. America's VetDogs specializes in placing highly skilled service and guide dogs to individuals with physical injuries, PTSD, hearing and vision loss, and seizures.

Their mission is to help those who have served our country honorably live with dignity and independence. All services are free, including transportation to and from our Smithtown, New York campus, instruction, and more.

In 2013, America's VetDogs became the second assistance dog school in the United States to be accredited by the International Guide Dog Federation and Assistance Dogs International; the Guide Dog Foundation was the first.

VetDogs has also been certified by PsychArmor, a national nonprofit that provides free education and support on how to work with, live with, or care for military veterans.

Accreditation and certification reinforce the organization's reputation by demonstrating that VetDogs consistently adheres to the highest standards for the humane and ethical treatment of dogs, maintains educational benchmarks for trainers and apprentices, and has procedures in place to support consumers throughout the application process, including a mechanism for addressing any grievances.

America's VetDogs was established by the Guide Dog Foundation for the Blind, Inc. in 2003 to provide assistance dogs to America's wounded veterans, helping them return to a life without boundaries. In 2006, it became a separate 501(c)(3) corporation; the two organizations continue to share staff and other resources to ensure people with disabilities receive the best services possible.

America's VetDogs has earned the Platinum Seal of Transparency from GuideStar/Candid. The Platinum Participant level requires that they share more than their financial data. They also report on goals, strategies, capabilities, and programs. VetDogs was also recognized by the Better Business Bureau Wise Giving Alliance as an accredited charity meeting their twenty "Standards for Charity Accountability." VetDogs has also been identified by The Patriots Initiative as an accredited charity that meets their best practices and most effectively supports our nation's armed forces communities.

More information is available at www.vetdogs.org,

at America's VetDogs
371 East Jericho Turnpike
Smithtown, NY 11787-2976

or by phone at 631-930-9000.

Warriors in Need (WIN)

What began as a fundraiser has evolved into a vital organization supporting veterans facing suicide and homelessness. WIN uses the skills of military veterans to fill the talent gap in the aviation industry. By connecting well-trained veterans to new jobs, WIN helps them build stable futures for themselves and their families, while maximizing the value of the training they've already received.

WIN's mission is to combat veteran suicide and homelessness by providing support for veterans as they successfully find their place in a new civilian life. As a veteran-owned 501(c)3 nonprofit, its foundation is rooted in the invaluable experiences gained through our CEO's service in the US Marine Corps. WIN's goal is to empower transitioning veterans and veterans with disabilities as they embark on a new chapter in civilian life.

Staggering rates of veteran suicide and homelessness persist, casting a shadow over the lives of individuals who embody the very best our nation has to offer. By rallying together, WIN and its supporters can provide the support these veterans deserve. WIN is dedicated to getting ahead of the issue and solving our problems.

Throughout our journeys, those who came before us have nurtured, educated, and guided us. We recognize that when we reach the pinnacle of our achievements, we must extend a helping hand to others. Warriors In Need serves as that beacon of support not only for its founder but for all who are willing and able to lend a hand. Together, we'll facilitate the transition, provide unwavering support, uplift, and sponsor veterans and disabled veterans as they turn the page on their military service and seamlessly integrate into civilian society.

More information can be found at www.warriorsinneed.com or reached at 747-946-1775.

If you are facing a crisis and do not know where to turn, please call the nationwide mental health lifeline at 988.

PTSD Foundation of America/Camp Hope

PTSD Foundation of America aims to bring hope and healing to veterans and families suffering from the effects of combat-related post-traumatic stress. This 501(c)(3) organization began as a grassroots effort in 2005 with a group of concerned volunteers searching for homeless veterans on the streets of Houston with a vision and passion for drastically reducing the veteran suicide rate through programming and outreach services.

In the past decade, 80,000 veterans were lost to suicide—20,000 more than the number of American soldiers killed in action in Vietnam. The Veterans Health Administration estimates that 22 veterans take their own lives daily. Through dedication to the mission, PTSD Foundation of America has successfully grown into a nationally recognized non-profit known for assisting combat veterans and their families with the complexities of post-traumatic stress, changing the trajectory of their lives, and transforming them into thriving and productive members of society.

Over the past twelve years, more than 16,000 combat veterans from all branches of the military and their families have found help, healing, and hope through our outreach program and at Camp Hope. These Outreach offices are in markets with some of the highest suicide rates among veterans. The PTSD Foundation of America has chapters in five states and six major cities, including Houston, San Antonio, Dallas, Atlanta, Phoenix, and Tampa. The primary goal in Outreach is to help veterans with PTSD and provide them with the Camp Hope program (if qualified), peer-to-peer services, warrior support groups, and crisis intervention. Outreach staff also supports local communities with PTSD and suicide awareness presentations to challenge them to get involved with veteran issues in their areas.

Since 2005, the PTSD Foundation of America has grown and adapted to meet combat veterans' (and their families') mental, physical, and spiritual needs. Camp Hope has facilitated over 350 group sessions with 4,321 attendees and provided over 3,000 in-person individual support meetings last year. Over the past decade, more than 1,800 combat veterans have found a renewed purpose, earned college degrees, secured employment, become financially independent, reunited with their families, and reintegrated into society.

For more information, please visit https://ptsdusa.org/, contact the PTSD Foundation of America/Camp Hope at 9724 Derrington Road, Houston, TX 77064, or call (832) 912-4429.

The Combat Trauma Help Line is 877-717-PTSD (7873).

Camp Hope

Camp Hope is a six- to nine-month interim housing program located in a quiet, safe setting in Houston, Texas, that aims to alleviate the effects of combat trauma through a comprehensive, whole-person approach. Its solution is to provide peer support, mentor programs, and professional development for America's warriors and their families. There is no cost for the veteran or their families in this first-of-its-kind program. The

Veterans also have weekly sessions with licensed healthcare professionals; to date, 44% of the veterans have graduated from the Camp Hope program.

Residents attend group lessons and support sessions with other combat veterans and are afforded individual mentoring sessions with certified combat trauma mentors. Participants may also take part in off-site interaction activities and trips, such as camping, fishing, and sporting events. Many are encouraged to get involved with local churches, businesses, and volunteer organizations to assist in their healing and educate the community on the invisible wounds of war.

The Camp Hope National Navigation team operates virtually to help veterans outside a 150-mile radius of Houston. National Navigation's services include warrior support groups, resource navigation, peer-to-peer mentoring, and logistical support for incoming and outgoing Camp Hope program residents.

Camp Hope Outreach chapters operate in markets with the highest suicide rates among veterans and provide on-site psychotherapy with licensed mental health clinicians specializing in addiction and trauma. Camp Hope helps to intervene with families, understanding that illness of any kind, especially mental illness, has a profound effect on the family system.

Camp Hope oversees each veteran's medical needs and coordinates community care, recognizing that in an integrated care system, veterans' spiritual needs are integral to their overall well-being and healing.

The Camp Hope Transition team bridges the gap between family members and their veterans while the veteran is a Camp Hope resident and after completing the program. The goal is to help the families navigate through their daily lives with a loved one who is dealing with signs and symptoms of PTSD by providing support, resources, and education, and by equipping families with the tools necessary, inspiring them to live a quality life filled with love, hope, purpose, and normality. PTSD affects not only the veteran but the whole family, and when the family is healed, the veteran has the best chance of succeeding.

Services provided include peer counseling, identifying resources and community support, support network development, education related to PTSD, substance abuse dependency, and co-dependency, empowering families to identify ways to make the necessary behavioral changes, and money management. More information is available at https://ptsdusa.org/camp-hope/.

Operation Song

Operation Song is a 501(c)(3) tax-exempt non-profit organization that empowers veterans, active-duty military members, and their families to tell their stories through songwriting. No musical or writing skills are required, only a willingness to share their stories and, with the help of professional songwriters, transform them into songs. Operation Song's vision is to honor and serve every veteran, military personnel, and their families through the power of songwriting and inspire every American with their stories.

Creating your song is a five-step process that begins with registering and reviewing the intake form. After review, you'll be paired with the right people to get things going. After writing, performing, and production, veterans will hear (and receive) their songs. Participants then become Operation Song alumni! Songwriters find a home in helping veterans, volunteers fulfill community outreach, and donors become part of a family. Learn more at https://op-song.squarespace.com/.

You may also contact Operation Song at PO Box 121746, Nashville, TN 37212-1746, call 844-967-7664, or e-mail contact@operationsong.org.

Family, Friends, and Normalcy

I retired during the 20th century, and since then, our area of conflict has shifted to Afghanistan and Iraq. Ahern et al. (2015) discussed and identified the challenges that Afghanistan and Iraq veterans face when transitioning from military to civilian life. The authors also offered approaches to recognizing and addressing these challenges. The veterans' experiences disrupted their connections with family and friends, as the sense of the military as a family doesn't always translate to the civilian, unstructured way of life.

Three themes arose from their research: the military as "family," "normal is alien," and searching for a "new" normal. The feeling of brotherhood and acceptance for who you are and what you are is often not found in the civilian, corporate, or academic worlds. The homecoming theory posits that veterans are separated from home, family, a familiar life, and time. Both the dependents at home and the veteran change during military service. All individuals are different during the transition period, compared to their prior service and during service. The expectations of transitioning and the reality are often vastly different, especially in the culture and environment (Ahern et al., 2015; Ainspan et al., 2018).

The feeling of the military as a family has two subthemes: caretaker and structure. The notion that the military takes care of its own and its members, exemplified by the phrase "I've got your six," is a common reality (Ahern et al., 2015). "No Soldier Left Behind" is more than a philosophy. It's a creed all members of the armed forces adhere to. Some leaders employ a parental aspect to their leadership style. Looking out for those under your command is nothing new; it is one of our primary responsibilities as leaders.

Mission first, people always. Veterans are accustomed to being responsible for the safety, training, and welfare of those under their command, as well as the care and support of those in their charge. This is also called "watching your back." This includes compassion and understanding for when "life" happens. Dropping in on one who may need food or resources until payday is one method of caring for each other (Ahern et al., 2015; Burke, 2023). Asking for help addressing mental health issues was seen as a sign of weakness while on active duty (Gordon et al., 2020). This attitude remains for many veterans upon discharge. This attitude also serves as a barrier to seeking help, thereby hindering the transition to civilian life.

The second subtheme was structure. The formality of the military day was marked by waking up with Reveille, having lunch at Mess Call, and hitting the rack at Taps.

The decisions and procedures were simple. The environment was described as "black and white," and instructions were given and followed (Ahern et al., 2015). Often, once back in the civilian world, the environment and acceptable social structure suddenly require transitioning veterans to be responsible for themselves and life tasks and responsibilities. The military has instructed them on what to do and how to do it. Veterans no longer lived in barracks or base housing. They now had to pay rent or a mortgage, something they had not had to do before.

Family and fraternal support are essential to successfully transitioning to the academic or civilian world and way of life. Many aspects of fraternal organizations, whether academic (for me, it was Kappa Kappa Psi) or veteran-focused (for me, it was the Student Veterans of America, or SVA), were influenced by the military. The most common are feelings of belonging, purpose, and self-worth. The struggles veterans face with a lack of purpose or structure upon discharge from the military and their return to academic or civilian life are essential issues in research for veterans (Ahern et al., 2015; Burke, 2023, 2022a, 2022b). With such struggles, it is difficult for veterans to realize "normal is alien," which leads to a search for a "new normal" (Ahern et al., 2015).

Returning to civilian life, veterans experience feelings of alienation and detachment from friends, family, and society. However, due to changes in military service, many aspects of civilian life are no longer relevant-they're alien to the veteran. The theme "normal is alien" had four subthemes: disconnection, unsupportive institutions, lack of structure, and loss of purpose (Ahern et al., 2015; Ainspan et al., 2018). Veterans often feel that they can no longer access their original family and social networks, and access to their service life is cut off, making it challenging to establish civilian networks. Participants experienced feelings of inadequacy and a loss of meaning due to uncertainty about their role. Learning how to integrate and interact within the civilian environment, with different social norms, was unfamiliar (Gordon et al., 2020).

Peer-to-Peer Suggested Methodologies

Ways to cope using the five senses. Five things to see, four things to hear, three to smell, two to touch, and one to taste. I recall the adage, but I don't remember the source. It may have been a common theme among my various classes. I first heard this as a kid living at home from one of my aunts. I thought it was funny at the time, because of the countdown - five down to one. I remember it because of the last line: one thing to taste. It was always delicious, but as usual, I'm digressing.

Individual intervention (1:1 chilling together), the VA calls this 1:1 Peer Intervention. Ahern et al. (2015)

concluded that the support veterans provide to one another is more often effective. Peer support may be a critical part of a successful transition, as veterans help one another and civilians understand the veteran experience. Given the long-term risk to those who experience an unsuccessful transition, it is essential to support veterans in transition. Peer groups, even the 1:1 group, need consistent interaction. Regularly scheduled meetings are essential for the success of 1:1 peer-to-peer interventions (Blackwell-Starnes, 2018).

Social support can affect the transition process. A positive support system was the most impactful aspect of navigating a successful transition (Shue et al., 2021). Supportive leadership enabled service members to prepare for life after military service. Conversely, poor support from military leadership will hinder successful transitioning. Social support is often regarded as an essential element to a successful transition. Veterans indicated their family and friends were vital to their success (Shue et al., 2021).

Research supports the benefits of veteran peer support specialists as an essential part of a treatment plan. Veterans reported increased social and emotional support, reduced stigma, and improved adherence to their treatment plans (McCormick et al., 2019). The shame of needing help is alleviated when speaking with a brother or sister who "has been there." The everyday previous life holds a bond. Veterans may not want to talk about their demons from serving and are reluctant to seek help. Veterans do not always feel they deserve to "get better" or may distrust the VA and their healthcare providers (McCormick et al., 2019).

Providing veterans with opportunities to develop peer relationships helps them feel a sense of belonging to the university, facilitating a smoother transition into the classroom. Creating social groups specifically for veterans with PTSD or for disabled student veterans helps student veterans support one another. This support and awareness that they are not alone in their transition develop a sense of belonging. This sense of belonging is a crucial aspect of transitioning to academic life. Developing a sense of belonging to the classroom is essential for their educational success (Blackwell-Starnes, 2018).

Veterans who connect socially have been found to have lower PTSD symptoms and suicide rates. Veterans with higher social connectedness have been associated with adaptive interpersonal skills, actively seeking to belong to the social world, and happiness. Connecting socially is crucial for understanding veterans' identification and well-being following their transition to civilian life (Flack & Kite, 2021).

Veterans often sought and found connections with other veterans through employment. Veterans also reported having support from family, friends, spouses/significant others, and their church (Keeling, 2018). Many veterans prefer and receive help via self-help and online services (Bond et al., 2020).

Grounding techniques help individuals "ground" themselves when they become overwhelmed. They can assist veterans in remaining in the present moment instead of becoming overwhelmed by traumatic memories and feelings. Grounding techniques work by helping veterans focus on what they observe in their environment by incorporating their senses. This may facilitate a connection with the present moment, detaching the veteran from past feelings and memories, and enabling them to address stressful stimuli later (Shield et al., 2020).

Breathing techniques may be taught to veterans, often with little thought to the exercise process. Becoming aware of one's breathing may aid in regulating one's emotions. By learning to breathe deeply, veterans automatically take in more oxygen and exhale more carbon dioxide, causing their bodies to relax and enter a calm state. This is particularly beneficial for veterans who experience overwhelming feelings (Shields et al., 2020).

Social Media

Pages/groups/chats/podcasts. Social media platforms make connecting easy to do: push a button. The VSOs discussed in this manuscript have ways to connect via several social media platforms: scroll to the bottom of their home page, and there you are! Go on a social media platform and type a search parameter in the search bar (veterans, PTSD, military, service-specific, etc.), and various groups and pages will pop up based on your subject input. YouTube, Facebook, and LinkedIn offer platforms to launch podcasts or video channels, as well as list several veteran-based groups and pages/organizations to follow. The search bar will display several results for you to select from, based on your search criteria.

Mobile apps have become an increasingly available resource for supporting veterans' transition process (Ainspan et al., 2018). Mental health doctors, assistance from a crisis line, and other resources are available online, via computer, laptop, or smartphone. The VA offers an app for easy access. Your records and communication with your health team are now at your fingertips.

Team Rubicon

Team Rubicon is not an SVO, as are the other agencies discussed. It's a veteran-led humanitarian organization that serves global communities before, during, and after disasters and crises. Their vision is to support humanity and build resiliency for vulnerable communities worldwide. Many veterans working or volunteering for Team Rubicon discover their sense of purpose.
Learn more information at
https://teamrubiconusa.org/about-us/.

Institute for Veterans & Military Families (IVMF)

IVMF is a veteran service organization on campus at Syracuse University. It is located at the National Veterans Resource Center, Daniel & Gayle D'Aniello Building, 101 Waverly Ave, Syracuse, NY 13244, or by phone at 315-443-0141.

IVMF at Syracuse University is higher education's first interdisciplinary academic institute, singularly focused on advancing the post-service lives of the nation's military veterans and their families, serving those who have served. Their mission is to empower service members, veterans, and their families through actionable research, innovative programs, and insightful analytics.

Syracuse University has a historic commitment to serving veterans and their families. The founding of the D'Aniello Institute for Veterans and Military Families in 2011 expanded that commitment to serve across the country and beyond.

Supported by a world-class advisory board and both public and private partners, their professional staff delivers unique and innovative career, vocational, and entrepreneurship education and training programs to transitioning service members, veterans, and military spouses. IVMF provides actionable and nationally impactful research, policy analysis, and program evaluation. It works with communities and non-profits nationwide to enhance service delivery for the 19 million veterans throughout the United States and their families.

More information is available at
https://ivmf.syracuse.edu/.

Chapter 5

The Journey

My journey has been a tumultuous one. I faced many challenges; however, one specific incident was my wake-up call, which led me on the path in a positive direction. The turning point for me was when I had a gun held up to my back in my driveway while my roommate was getting his butt kicked, as "disrespecting Pete's house by bringing business where it does not belong" was being screamed repeatedly as the blows were being administered. Bringing business to my place was a disrespect to my house, and, apparently, to me. It was a strange experience. I was going to deliver some whoop-ass to the guys beating up my roommate, but then it was suggested that I don't move. "Click-click." I knew then that I had to get my shit together. I shut my roommate down, evicted him, and stayed alive. I started to think about going back to school, but I also knew I needed help and was desperate for the right kind of support system. I was looking for a new normal.

Searching for a "new normal" involved support from a navigator (a mentor or peer advisor), embracing an ambassador role, and the realization the challenges of transition are inevitable but should diminish over time (Ahern et al., 2015). I found a "navigator" late in my transition, Kappa Kappa Psi, beginning in 1997, and SVA around 2022. I didn't have individual mentors; I had organizations. It would've been different for someone who was retired by age 34 to have a traditional student as a mentor. Due to my age and experience, I slipped into an ambassador role. I was a chapter leader in my fraternity and actively involved in the community through music.

While actively involved with Kappa Kappa Psi and my music (composing, conducting, performing), I felt closest to being myself, but I knew something was a tad off. I retired and went to school a year later. My active participation with Kappa Kappa Psi spanned from my undergraduate studies at Cameron University to my graduate school years at the University of Oklahoma. It faded when I moved to Missouri.

During my time in Missouri, away from my music and not yet involved with SVA, I grew increasingly more aware of things being "off" within me. I was not very involved with my passion, music. Thankfully, I started seeing my VA primary care provider once a year. My sense of self and being part of a brotherhood were diminishing, but my brothers and sisters were always with me. They've always been a part of me.

I moved to Tennessee in 2016 for a job in music education. I was returning to music, but now I'd be teaching. I was excited! Unfortunately, this opportunity didn't work out as I expected. I ended up as a substitute teacher for a year and a half. Once the curriculum went online, I was no longer a teacher- I was a glorified babysitter, saying, "Get off YouTube and back on Google Classroom." I resigned my position as a babysitter in the public school system. I was losing my sense of self again.

When I arrived in Tennessee, a friend and I ate at a local fast-food place. While there, my hyperawareness was evident. I felt anxious, and my nerves kept me alert. My friend asked whether I was making a threat assessment or "getting ready to blow up the place." Again, a few days later, at a Mexican restaurant, the same scenario. At this point, I'd been away from Kappa Kappa Psi for a short time and hadn't yet found SVA. I was searching for my sense of purpose once again.

I discovered SVA in 2021- I'd followed them on social media and LinkedIn and found a sense of purpose. I attended my first SVA National Conference (NatCon) in 2023, the 15th Anniversary of SVA in Florida.

As I transition, I've noticed changes in myself and my circumstances. I recall presenting at the SVA NatCon 2023. It was an example of immersion therapy, as it were. I was jumping in with both feet, all while shaking like a leaf. My nerves and anxiety got the better of me, as I completed my 25-minute presentation in less than 12 minutes. Despite my speedy talk, the session was successful. It featured lots of information exchange and individuals connecting. I was happy with the result, but didn't feel I'd be asked to present again. My anxiety and nerves won that round.

My next year at NatCon was better, not only for me but also for my nerves and anxiety. I wasn't a presenter. I was an attendee, one of thousands. I even attended a concert at the Grand Ole Opry. Being among so many people pushed me out of my comfort zone. The redeeming thing was that I was among other veterans attending. I actually felt like myself during my time at the NatCons.

During Washington Week in 2024, I met many new student veterans. We were there to be heard in Washington, D.C., to give our voice on veterans' issues. While in the antechamber, a fellow student veteran noticed I looked a bit pale. Wow, this was fantastic! I didn't realize that my nerves were making their presence known. I was told that I should get some air or some water. I was offered a buddy walk, but the latrine was a short distance away, so I declined. I only had to cut my way through the crowd. Quickly enough, I had no problem getting to the latrine. Such was the parting of the Red Sea.

I was being looked out for without even realizing it. That is what we, veterans, do. We have each other's six. We moved into the Senate hearing, and I found being in such an open space relieved some of my anxiety. The historical implications of the hearing and the beauty of the setting made me feel proud to be a part of the legislative process. I felt a sense of purpose. I felt like myself.

During my time with SVA, I've noticed a growing movement within the VA and higher education to acknowledge veterans' unseen wounds and ease their transition from military to civilian life.

The "Feeling"

My transition journey is still in progress. Sometimes, I park at a scenic view for a few minutes, but eventually move on.

I have transitioned from military to civilian, with a "year of hell" before transitioning to student-veteran. As a student-veteran, I'm nontraditional due to my age, retirement, and veteran status. Then, I transitioned to being a married student-veteran with children. I attended CU for my Bachelor of Music and Master of Arts degrees.

My next transition as a student-veteran was as a single parent in graduate school at OU for my Master of Music Education degree, after my second wife left and moved to New England. I transitioned to a single-parent student-veteran during my first year. Upon graduation in 2011, I transitioned again. This time towards being a veteran civilian. During this period, I was unable to hold a job for very long. I moved out of state to find employment, only to discover (after I had moved) that they had hired someone else. So, I was unemployed and looking for work. I returned to school to get "qualified" for more positions in higher education. I was now transitioning to being a student-veteran again.

I moved to a new state in 2016, during my doctoral studies, hoping to secure a new teaching position. The district hired me; however, the schools did not pick me up, as I was "too expensive" for their budget. I held other jobs, but again, not for long. I enjoyed my jobs and had a sound work acquaintance/work friend support system. Those jobs did not last, and I wound up unemployed again. In December of 2024, I eventually retired for good.

I'm still in transition. I genuinely enjoy my affiliation with Kappa Kappa Psi, its sister sorority Tau Beta Sigma, and SVA. I would come out of "retirement" to work remotely or in person with either organization. I find myself and my sense of purpose when I play my instruments or conduct music; I prefer to be in front of an ensemble. I find a sense of purpose when I engage in activities with Kappa Kappa Psi and Tau Beta Sigma, as well as local and national events with SVA. When I do so, I feel like my old self. I feel like "Sarge," as I was affectionately nicknamed. Do I know how, when, or where my transition will be complete? No, I do not. However, I'm looking forward to continuing the journey.

Chapter 6

Other Veterans' Experiences—Your Story Matters!

This chapter features stories submitted by other veterans. I hope these stories inspire you. The stories are presented in the order they were received.

To all who see these presents, greetings! The following veterans have submitted their stories: Caitlyn Van Dam, SGT, USMC; Omar Reynoso, SFC, U.S. Army (Ret.); Ralph Figueroa, CPL, U.S. Army; and Shena R. Veale, SSG, U.S. Army.

May their stories inspire and motivate you.

Caitlyn Van Dam

Name: Caitlyn Van Dam

Rank: E-5 Sergeant

Branch of Service: United States Marine Corps

MOS: 7041 Aviation Operations Specialist (Operations Chief)

Years of Service: 7 years 11 months

Poverty. Abuse. Drugs. These were not distant headlines or cautionary tales; they were my reality. My name is Caitlyn, and I was a poor Latina girl in secondhand clothes. Growing up, my mom moved us constantly. She did what she could, but stability was never within reach. We bounced between towns and across states, always in communities forgotten by institutions and dismissed by society. I was just getting started in life, and already the world had decided how my story would end.

But the world did not know me, not yet anyway, and that would not be my ending. I had a fire and a sense of purpose. I knew I was meant for more, that I could rise above my circumstances and not succumb to the life I was born into. At fifteen, I moved in with my father, and three years later, I joined the United States Marine Corps.

I served my country for eight years, completed two deployments, was meritoriously promoted three times, and received numerous awards for performance and leadership. I held my own and often outperformed my male counterparts in a demanding, male-dominated field. I led with grit, resilience, and discipline.

What I did not mention is that when I was nine years old, my stepfather told me I was going to be an architect. At the time, I did not understand the weight of his words, but they stayed with me. The way I observed the world, as a curious and detail-oriented person, suddenly made sense.

At the seven-year mark in my service, I stood at a crossroads. I had been selected for promotion to Staff Sergeant, one of the greatest honors in my military career. However, a last-minute policy change made the promotion contingent on extending my contract by fifteen months. I had already decided to end my active service at the end of my second enlistment to attend university and pursue a master's degree. I walked away without the rank I had worked incredibly hard for. I left the Marine Corps with a bitterness that weighed on me.

My transition into civilian life was nothing short of overwhelming. I had a newborn in my arms and a lifetime of uncertainty ahead of me. We had just moved from Hawaii to South Dakota, a place I had never lived, far from anything familiar. I had no family nearby, no support system of my own, just my spouse and his family. And only three months after leaving the Marine Corps, I started college. I was older than most of my classmates. I was more mature. I was a mother. I was a Marine… and I was utterly lost.

I had never felt more out of place than when I did on my first day of class. My priorities, worldview, and interests vastly differed from those of my classmates. I felt the need to blend in, so I shrank into the background. I let fear and insecurity consume me. I made no friends that first year. But I did not let that bring me down. I focused on my infant daughter. I was breastfeeding and navigating challenging courses. That was where I placed my energy.

As the years passed, something became very clear: I care deeply about the military community. I accepted that I was feeling disconnected, isolated, and alone from my peers in uniform. My school is not active with Student Veterans of America events, so I did not discover the organization until someone encouraged me to apply for the SVA Leadership Institute. A few weeks later, I was accepted into the seminar.

That experience changed everything.

I stopped hiding. I began advocating for military-affiliated students. I started speaking about my experiences and incorporating my knowledge into my academic work. My projects became reflections of what I truly cared about. I came to realize that what made me different was my greatest asset. I lived a different life. I have a story to tell. I have value.

I still miss my military community, but I am actively pursuing opportunities to reconnect with it. I am seeking roles that enable me to serve, give back, and lead. Politics and architecture are my passions. It has taken me nearly four years post-service to discover that intersection, but I have found it.

I discovered programs that transition service members into the congressional world. I applied and found success. Although I could not accept the position, it reaffirmed that I belong in this space. I have been inducted into the Tau Sigma Delta and Phi Kappa Phi honor societies. I secured an architectural internship, an opportunity I credit, in part, to the leadership and work ethic instilled in me by the Marine Corps.

So now, despite countless obstacles, many of which remain untold, that poor Latina girl from the south side of town will soon graduate with her master's degree. Moreover, she will do so with honors. It is a milestone that I once felt impossible.

I am a mother, a lifelong learner, a leader, a creative thinker, and an advocate. To many, I am Sergeant Coscarelli. Furthermore, I will always be a United States Marine.

Omar Reynoso

Name: Omar Reynoso

Rank: Sergeant First Class (SFC)

Branch of Service: US Army

MOS: 38B (2008-2022) (Civil Affairs Specialist), 15U (2001-2008) (CH-47 Mechanic), 68W (1994-2001) (Combat Medic)

Years of Service: 28

Hi. My name is Omar Reynoso, and this is my story.

The transition had been long and arduous. For Sergeant First Class (SFC) Omar Reynoso, the military had been his entire life since preadolescence, when he enlisted in the Army Reserves at 17 — a structured world with clear expectations and a defined purpose. The first year after retirement was the hardest, adrift in the civilian sea, like a paratrooper without a helmet. His DD-214, the certificate of release or discharge from active duty, felt less like a badge of honor and more like a permission slip into a bewildering new reality.

Years before retiring, one of his coworkers told him what he needed to prepare for retirement (medical records in order, finances straight, education, TAPS, etc.). he attended multiple programs (Commit Foundation, Centurion Military Alliance, Leader Transition Institute, FourBlock, The Honor Foundation, and American Corporate Partners) that helped veterans translate their military skills into civilian qualifications. Omar, initially skeptical, decided to give it a try. He discovered that his expertise was highly sought after. His leadership experience, framed in the context of team building and non-profit, finally resonated with potential employers. He thought he was on the right track…

It was the silence that struck SFC Reynoso first. After twenty-eight years of the cacophony of military life – the predawn reveille, physical fitness in the morning, the movement in the office, the constant meetings, the rhythmic cadence of marching boots in ceremonies – the quiet of his home felt unnerving, almost hostile like the enemy. He'd traded his uniform for slacks and a polo, his M4 for a keyboard, and the unwavering camaraderie of his unit for the isolating hum of his laptop.

Job hunting and interviews proved to be a demoralizing exercise. His extensive leadership experience, honed through countless deployments, and his unwavering discipline seemed to translate poorly onto civilian resumes. Employers nodded politely, impressed by his service, but ultimately hired candidates with "relevant industry experience". The unspoken question hung in the air: What exactly did you do in the military that we can use here?

Then there was the healthcare. During his time in uniform, medical care had been seamless, readily available, and comprehensive. Tricare had been a constant, a reliable safety net. Now, navigating this labyrinth of VA, Tricare, and civilian health insurance felt like deciphering an alien language. He'd applied for VA benefits, a process that involved countless medical records and frustrating delays. Meanwhile, a persistent ache in his lower back, a souvenir from years of carrying a rucksack, jumping out of planes, and flight duty, flared with increasing intensity.

He tried to ignore it, attributing it to the unfamiliar softness of his civilian mattress. But the pain worsened, radiating to the other side and down his leg. Simple tasks, such as yard work and walking to the mailbox, became an ordeal. He managed to schedule an appointment at his local VA clinic within a few weeks, thanks to the excellent care team at the clinic. He remembered the immediate access to medical professionals during deployments, his team medic who could patch him up in the field. Now, you will undergo X-rays and labs, see your primary care physician (PCM), receive physical therapy, and then proceed to whatever comes next (surgery?). This process takes time to get used to.

Loneliness gnawed at him. His family was his rock, their unwavering support a lifeline in this turbulent period. However, they couldn't fully understand the void left by the absence of his military family. The shared experiences and the unspoken understanding forged in the crucible of deployments were unique and irreplaceable. He missed the late-night talks in the office, the shared anxieties before a mission, the boisterous celebrations after a successful one. Civilian friendships felt… different, lacking the deep-seated trust and shared history.

He found himself isolated and angry, retreating into the familiar silence of his home. The news played in the background, a constant reminder of the world he had sworn to protect, a world he now felt disconnected from as it moved along without him. Doubt began to creep in. Had he made the right decisions? Was he even capable of adapting to this new life?

One particularly difficult day, the back pain was so severe he could barely move. Frustration boiled over. He slammed his fist on the table, the echo amplifying the emptiness of the room. His son Alec found him hunched over, his face etched with pain and despair.

"Dad," he said softly, standing beside him. He consoled him. It reminded him that he's not alone in this. Helped put into perspective the saying, "The struggle is real" and "you've got this."

His love and presence were a balm to his wounded spirit. He finally admitted the depth of his physical, mental, and emotional pain. He navigated the VA system, sought care through different programs (Defenders of Freedom and Operation Mend), advocating for appointments and pushing through the pain. His family became his tireless advocate, proving invaluable in a world he no longer understood.

Slowly, things began to shift. He connected with a local veterans' support group. Sharing his experiences with others who had walked a similar path was cathartic. He found a sense of belonging again, a shared understanding that transcended civilian life. They swapped stories of bureaucratic battles, job search woes, and the lingering echoes of their time in service.

He began attending networking events, both in-person and virtual, such as The K.E.Y. and Vets2Industry, where he learned the nuances of civilian business culture and tailored his resume to highlight transferable skills. The process was still challenging, but for the first time since leaving the military, Omar felt a flicker of hope.

The healthcare journey was still ongoing. After months of appointments, chiropractor visits, and Stretch Zone sessions, his back pain began to subside. He learned to navigate the VA system, understanding its limitations and advocating for his needs. He also realized the importance of connecting with other veterans who had successfully navigated the healthcare landscape. Their shared knowledge and support were invaluable.

One day, he received a call offering him a position as a veteran service officer for the state of Florida. The interviewers had been impressed not only by his skills and discipline but by his passion for volunteering and helping others. It wasn't the same as leading his team, but it offered a sense of purpose and a chance to utilize his hard-earned skills to help care for veterans and their families.

Omar Reynoso's transition was far from seamless. It was a journey marked by frustration, loneliness, and the daunting reality of navigating a world vastly different from the one he had known for so long. However, through perseverance, the unwavering support of his family, and the camaraderie of his fellow veterans, he began to find his footing. The silence in his home still lingered, but now it was often punctuated by the sounds of his work calls, the laughter shared with family, and the quiet satisfaction of building a new life, brick by hard-earned brick. The uniform was gone, but the strength, resilience, and unwavering spirit forged in his years of service remained, guiding him toward a new definition of success in the civilian world.

Ralph Figueroa

Name: Ralph Figueroa

Rank: CPL

Branch of Service: U.S. Army

MOS: 13E (Cannon Fire Direction Specialist)

Years of Service: 1994-2006 (12 years)

From the Military to the Books: My Journey of Transition, Grit, and Growth

My name is Ralph Figueroa, and I am a proud U.S. Army veteran. Transitioning from the military to civilian life is rarely a straight path, and my journey has been anything but conventional. I joined the Army at just 17 years old, a young, motivated, and determined individual eager to build a better life through discipline and service. At 21, now serving in the Army National Guard, I began college at Cal Poly Pomona. I had big dreams of earning a degree and becoming a teacher, but the pressure of being a full-time student while working six hours a day eventually became overwhelming. At that time, there were no veteran support services on campus, and I lacked the guidance and structure I was accustomed to in the military. By the fall of 2000, I dropped out, unsure if I would ever return.

To gain financial independence and stability, I entered the collision repair industry. Starting as an apprentice, I quickly climbed the ladder, becoming a parts manager and eventually an estimator, one of the most sought-after roles in the field due to the potential for high earnings. My work ethic, forged in the military, helped me earn respect and promotions. However, when my unit was called up in 2003 and again in 2004, everything paused, and my entire life pivoted in a direction I was not ready for. After being honorably discharged in 2006, I returned to the only industry I knew, eventually becoming a body shop manager. It was something I was really good at, but I also knew that this was never my true calling.

In 2010, after nearly a decade in the auto industry, I was laid off due to budget cuts. I'm not going to lie, did that one really hurt. That blow was tough to take, but it led me to something entirely new and completely unexpected. A month later, I pivoted into the entertainment world, producing shows, hosting events, and even performing for the troops stationed around the world as a standup comedian. For the next ten years, I succeeded in that field, using the same traits the military had instilled in me: discipline, resilience, and adaptability.

Yet, despite the creative highs, something remained unfinished—the promise I made to myself when I enlisted—to earn my college degree. No matter how successful I was or how much money I earned, it always lingered in the back of my mind.

In 2020, at the age of 43, I made the bold decision, and to be honest, a scary one at that, to go back to college and finish what I had started. I re-enrolled and was accepted at Cal Poly Pomona in February 2020, unaware that COVID-19 would soon shake the world to its core. While many saw the pandemic as a setback, I viewed it as an opportunity to focus. I leaned into my strengths: grit, time management, and leadership. For two straight academic years, I earned nothing but A's and graduated cum laude in May 2022 with a Bachelor of Arts in Liberal Studies. It was the moment I had envisioned over two decades earlier, finally realized, except I really didn't feel accomplished because deep down, I knew I could do more. Time to go big or go home, so I decided not to stop there.

I had applied and was eventually accepted into the Master of Arts program in Rehabilitation Counseling at California State University, San Bernardino (CSUSB), where I thrived academically and professionally. Balancing coursework, fieldwork, leadership roles, and family life wasn't easy. However, I applied the same organizational skills and discipline I had used as a soldier and manager, giving it all I had. I threw the impostor syndrome out the window, and despite feeling like the chips were stacked against me, I went all in and began my grad program in the fall of 2022.

In hindsight, the best decision I made was to resurrect the CSUSB Student Veterans Organization (SVO). Little did I know what doors would open because of that choice. The SVO board and I got to work, and through our collective efforts, we created the VSC Food/Snack Pantry, the SVO Math Coaching Initiative, the CSUSB Veterans Round Table, and the SVO Hygiene Commissary, which offered hygiene products at no cost to students. Our club was doing big things on our campus, not only helping student veterans and their families, but also every student who set foot in the Veterans Success Center (VSC). The SVO was eventually named the 2023-2024 Student Club of the Year at CSUSB. We also discovered Student Veterans of America (SVA) shortly after we chartered the SVO, and boy, we're so grateful we did. We dove right in and got involved in our community, attending NatCon. I was selected for the 2024 SVA Leadership Institute and received the John Edelman Scholars Scholarship.

Just when I thought things couldn't get any better, in January of 2025, exactly one year after attending our first SVA NatCon, I was honored as the SVA Student Veteran of the Year! Not going to lie, I didn't see that coming, but that motivated me to work even harder and keep going. A month later, I was appointed by my county supervisor as a Commissioner on the San Bernardino County Veterans Advisory Committee. In May 2025, I graduated with my master's degree, earning a 4.0 GPA, and while also passing the national certification exam. Sure, I accomplished some incredible milestones, but my sleeves are rolled up because I still have work to do, and with the support of my family, mentors, and colleagues, I will continue educating, inspiring, and advocating on behalf of veterans nationwide at the highest levels. The next transition is on the horizon, but this time around, I am extremely excited about the incredible opportunities it will create, as they will enable me to fully support my family and give them the life they deserve. That is where my true happiness and motivation lie…my family.

Looking back, my success didn't come from luck; it came from leaning into what I learned in the military: how to lead, how to adapt, and how to persist. My transitions, both from service to civilian life and later from working professional to student, were grounded in resilience and a passion to help others. I took pride in asking for help, building community, and creating structure in chaotic environments. That mindset helped me excel not only in the classroom but also in leadership roles within the Student Veterans Organization and the Veterans Success Center at my college campus.

For student veterans facing similar transitions, I offer these tips: 1) Embrace your military strengths—they're ASSETS in school and work. 2) Get organized and manage your time wisely. 3) Don't be afraid to ask for help by seeking out campus veteran centers, mentors, and counselors. 4) Build a support system. Community and camaraderie make the journey less isolating, and you'll need all the support you can get. 5) Most importantly, stay focused on your mission! Your purpose, your "why," will carry you through the hard days. The path won't be easy, but with grit, planning, and a willingness to grow, success is not only possible, it's yours to take. Now go get it!

Shena R. Veale

Name: Shena R. Veale

Rank: Staff Sergeant (SSG)

Branch of Service: United States Army

MOS: 25U (Signal Support Systems Specialist)

Years of Service: 26 years (20 in the Alabama National Guard, Active Duty since 2019).

"Purpose doesn't end with a DD-214—it evolves."

I was 17 when I joined the U.S. Army. For me, the uniform wasn't just about service—it was about becoming someone strong enough to protect others. I was raised primarily by my grandmother, alongside my sisters, brother, aunts, uncles, cousins, foster family, and church family. I knew early on what instability and responsibility looked like. My mother struggled with alcoholism, yet I've always honored her for her loving and selfless spirit. She visited when she could, and her warmth remains one of the earliest forms of love I ever felt. It's important to me that her struggle does not define her story, but by the deep heart she always gave.

Now with 26 years of service behind me—20 in the Alabama National Guard and on active duty since 2019—I've experienced the full spectrum of military life. I've served in homeland security, disaster recovery, hurricane relief, and combat deployments. Currently, I serve as an instructor at Fort Eisenhower and as the Unit Public Affairs Representative for the U.S. Army Signal School. I teach Soldiers more than just communication—I teach life lessons about growth, grit, and purpose. I use analogies, storytelling, and reframing to help others understand the power of resilience and the importance of emotional growth. On one particularly difficult deployment, where the heat was relentless and downtime was rare, I bought a $12 hammock and used my half-days off to rest with my Bible, headphones, or a simple game. That small ritual became my "reset button." I now remind Soldiers that the Army may not always offer compassion, but we can still care for ourselves. Even short, intentional moments of rest can restore clarity and strength. I'm far from perfect, and my journey has had many challenges and lessons. I'm grateful for every step that brought me here.

Outside of my military duties, I remain actively involved in organizations that support the military and veteran communities. I was honored to serve as a 2024 Shero Coffee Club Ambassador and continue to support the sisterhood through ongoing promotions, podcasts, articles, and more. Shero Coffee Club is a powerful community founded to support women veterans through connection, healing, and shared stories. I also serve on the leadership board for Operation Teammate, an organization that provides mentorship and unforgettable experiences for military children by connecting them with athletes. Additionally, I contribute to the Women Veterans Calendar project, which honors and highlights the stories of female service members nationwide. These efforts allow me to give back to the communities that have shaped and supported me, and ensure others feel seen, celebrated, and never alone.

I'm deeply thankful for the leaders and peers who invested their time and wisdom in me throughout my career—without them, I wouldn't be where I am today. Their support helped shape my leadership style and instilled in me a deep appreciation for giving back, especially when no one's watching. That's why I created a mentorship program for Soldiers preparing for higher levels of responsibility. I created this program not because I have all the answers, but because I want to share what I've learned and continue growing alongside others. It's also why I continue to advocate for military children, support women veterans, and stay actively involved in veteran service organizations. I never want anyone—especially those who've served—to feel forgotten or alone.

My connection to family has always been central to who I am. The love and strength of my grandmother and sister grounded me during difficult times. My grandmother's voice, steady and sure, still echoes in my mind when I'm facing tough choices. However, along the way, I've also found family in the communities I've served—battle buddies, mentees, fellow veterans, and even strangers who became lifelong friends through shared experiences. Whether in uniform or out, that extended family—built on shared purpose and mutual respect—has become just as sacred to me as blood ties.

While I still have six years until I transition, I've already begun preparing. I haven't enrolled in the Transition Assistance Program (TAP) yet, but I've spent time exploring what it offers. TAP isn't just for the final chapter of service—it's a toolkit that helps ease the hard pivot from military to civilian life by providing resources like resume writing, interview prep, translating military skills into civilian language, understanding VA benefits, mental health resources, and career placement. Several friends of mine are currently participating in internships offered through the Army. The Army Career Skills Program offers job training and internships during the last 180 days of service. It's something I plan to fully engage with when the time comes.

In the meantime, I strongly encourage fellow service members to take the initiative. Don't wait until the final year. Attend job fairs. Show up at conferences. Join veteran groups. These experiences build your network, open unexpected doors, and help create a foundation for life beyond the uniform. These early steps may feel uncertain, even lonely, but you're not just transitioning from a job—you're stepping into a new mission. Like many, I'm still learning how to navigate this next chapter, and I encourage fellow service members to support one another as we figure it out together.

Working at the ID card office gave me a firsthand look at how many veterans carry a sense of loss, isolation, or uncertainty after leaving the service. That time reminded me how critical it is to stay connected—and how much power there is in simply being present for one another. Spend a few minutes with a veteran when you see one—

what may seem like nothing in the moment may be everything to them.

As I continue to serve, I'm also preparing for what's next with intention. I believe the end of a military career is not the end of purpose—it's just a shift in how we serve. Every day, I'm reminded that no matter how much experience I have, there's always room to grow, give back, and learn from those around me, whether or not they outrank me.

"This life is too short—forgive often, keep learning, show gratitude, be kind, and love 🖤 like your life depends on it."

References

Ahern J., Worthen M., Masters J., Lippman SA., Ozer EJ., & Moos R. (2015). The challenges of Afghanistan and Iraq veterans' transition from military to civilian life and approaches to reconnection. *PLOS ONE*, *10*(7): e0128599.
https://doi.org/10.1371/journal.pone.0128599

Ainspan, N.D., Penk, W., & Kearney, L. K. (2018). Psychological approaches to improving the military-to-civilian transition process. *Psychological Services*, *15*(2), 129-134. https://dx.doi.org/10.1037/ser0000259

ASHE (2011). What Matters to Veterans? Peer Influences and the Campus Environment. ASHE Higher Education Report, 37(3), 21–33.
http://www.mentalhealth.va.gov/studentveteran/vital.asp.

Blackwell-Starnes, K. (2018). At ease: Developing veterans' sense of belonging in the college classroom. *Journal of Veterans Studies*, *3*(1). 18-36. https://journal-veterans-studies.org/articles/10.21061/jvs.v3i1.2

Blosnich, J. R., Montgomery, A. E., Dichter, M. E., Gordon, A. J., Kavalieratos, D., Taylow, L., Ketterer, B., & Bossarte, R. M. (2020). Social determinants and military veterans' suicide ideation and attempt: A cross-sectional analysis of electronic health record data. *J Gen Intern Med*, *35*(6), 1759-1767. DOI: 10.1007/s11606-019-05447-z

Bond, G. R., Al-Abdulmunem, M., Drake, R. E., Davis, L. L., Meyer, T., Gade, D. M., Frueh, B. C., Dickman, R. B., & Ressler, D. R. (2022). Transition from military service: Mental health and well-being among service members and veterans with service-connected disabilities. *The Journal of Behavioral Health Services Research*, *49*(3), pp. 282-298. DOI: 10.1007/s11414-021-09778-w

Burke, P. J. (2021). Perceptions of student-veterans with PTSD and availability of support services in academic life: A qualitative descriptive analysis (Order No. 28769510) [Doctoral dissertation, Northcentral University]. ProQuest Dissertations and Theses Global.

Burke, P. J. (2022a). Discovering Listed PTSD Support on Campus in Higher Education: A Web Survey of Traditional Academic Institution Home Pages. *Journal of Veterans Studies*, *8*(3), pp. DOI: https://doi.org/10.21061/jvs.v8i3.342 79-92.

Burke, P. J. (2022b). *A Student-Veteran's Experience with Higher Education: An Academic Journey.* Prominence Publishing: Amazon. ISBN: 978-1-990830-13-6.

Burke, P. J. (2023). *A Student-Veteran's Experience with Higher Education: Social, Family, and Fraternal Support…and Peppi, too!* Prominence Publishing: Amazon. ISBN: 978-1-990830-44-0.

Burke, P. J. (2024). *A Student-Veteran's Experience with Higher Education: The Musical Support.* Prominence Publishing: Amazon. ISBN: 978-1-990830-75-4.

Crone, B., Metraux, S., & Sbrocco, T. (2022). Health service access among homeless veterans: Health access challenges faced by homeless African American veterans. *Journal of Racial and Ethnic Health Disparities*, 9, pp. 1828-1844.
https://doi.org/10.1007/s40615-021-01119-z.

Dolan, G., McCauley, M., & Murphy, D. (2022). Factors influencing the salience of military/veteran identity post discharge: A scoping review. *Journal of Veteran Studies*, *8*(1), 231-246.
DOI: https://doi.org/10.21061/jvs.v8i1.333

Finnegan, A., & Randles, R. (2023). Prevalence of common mental health disorders in military veterans: Using primary healthcare data. *BMJ Military Health*, 169, pp. 523-528.
https://dx.doi.org/10.1136/bmjmilitary-2021-002045

Flack, M., and Kite, L. (2021). Transition from military to civilian: Identity, social connectedness, and veteran wellbeing. *PLoS ONE*, *16*(12): e0261634.
https://doi.org/10.1371/journal.pone.0261634

Garvin, L. A., Greenan, M. A., Edelman, E. J., Slightam, C., McInnes, D. K., & Zulman, D. M. (2023). Increasing use of video telehealth among veterans experiencing homelessness with substance use disorder: Design of a peer-led intervention. *Journal of Technology in Behavioral Science*, *8*, 234-245.
https://doi.org/10.1007/s41347-022-00290-2

Godier-McBard, L., Nicola G., and Fossey, M. (2021). We also served: The health and well-being of female veterans in the UK. *Anglia Ruskin Research Online* (ARRO). Report.
https://hdl.handle.net/10779/aru.23783757.v1

Gordon, K., Burnell, K., & Wilson, C. (2020). Outside the military "bubble": Life after service for UK ex-armed forces personnel. *Front. Public Health*, *8*(50).
Doi: 10.3389/fpubh2020.00050.

Jim-Suleiman, S., Ibiamke, A., & Fenan, N. V. (2021). A review of literature on the concept, motivations and factors affecting the success of veteran entrepreneurs. *European Journal of Accounting, Auditing and Finance Research*, *9*(4), 42-51. Online ISSN: 2053-4094

Keeling, M. (2018. Stories of transition: US veterans' narratives of transition to civilian life and the importance of identity. *Journal of Military, Veteran and Family Health*, *4*(2), 28-36.
Doi: 10.3138/jmvfh.2017-0009.

Kinney, A. R., Graham, J. E., & Eakman, A. M. (2020). Factors distinguishing veterans participating in supported education services from veterans on campus: Evidence supporting modifiable intervention targets. *Psychiatric Rehabilitation Journal*, *43*(3), 261-269.
https://psycnet.apa.org/record/2019-76862-001

Kirchner, M. J. (2015). Supporting student veteran transition to college and academic success. *Adult Learning*, *26*(3), 116–123.
https://doi.org/10.1177/1045159515583813

Kirchner, M. J., & Biniecki, S. M. Y. (2019). Student veteran career pathways: A proposed framework for higher education. *New Horizons in Adult Education & Human Resource Development*, *31*(2), 27–40.
https://journals.sagepub.com/doi/abs/10.1002/nha3.20248

Lee, J. E. C., Dursun, S., Skomorovsky, A. & Thompson, J. M. (2020). Correlates of perceived military to civilian transition challenges among Canadian Armed Forces Veterans. *Journal of Military, Veteran and Family Health*, *6*(2), 26-39.
doi: 10.3138/jmvfh-2019-0025

LePage, P. (2020). Retaining united states military veterans in the civilian workforce. *Muma Business Review*, *4*(9)91-106.
https://www.researchgate.net/profile/Patty-Lepage/publication/342852342_Retaining_United_States_Military_Veterans_in_the_Civilian_Workforce/links/5f0904ae299bf18816127698/Retaining-United-States-Military-Veterans-in-the-Civilian-Workforce.pdf

Maguire, A. M., Keyser, J., Brown, K., Kivlahan, D. Romaniuk, M., Gardner, I. R., & Dwyer, M. (2022). Veteran families with complex needs: A qualitative study of the veterans' support system. *Health Services Research*, *22*(74). https://doi.org/10.1186/s12913-021-07368-2

McCaslin, S. E., Thiede, J., Vinatieri, T., Passi, H., Lyon, K. B., Ahern, D. A., Armstrong, K., & Chitaphong, K. (2014). Facilitating veterans' academic success: Veterans Integration to Academic Leadership (VITAL) Initiative. *Career Planning & Adult Development Journal*, *30*(3), 191–209.

McCormick, W. H., Currier, J. M., Sims, B. M., Slagel, B. A., Carrol, T. D., Hamner, K., & Albright, D. L. (2019). Military culture and post-military transitioning among veterans: A qualitative analysis. *Journal of Veterans Studies*, *4*(2), 287-298. https://journal-veterans-studies.org/articles/10.21061/jvs.v4i2.121

Morgan, N. R., Aronson, K. R., Perkins, D. F., Bleser, J. A., Davenport, K., Vogt, D., Copeland, L. A., Finley, E. P., & Gilman, C. L. (2020). Reducing barriers to post-9/11 veterans' use of programs and services as they transition to civilian life. *BMC Health Services Research*. https://doi.org/10.1186/s12913-020-05320-4

Monteith, L. L., Holliday, R., Dichter, M. E., & Hoffmire, C. A. (2022). Preventing suicide among women veterans: Gender-sensitive, trauma-informed conceptualization. *Curr Treat Options Psych*, 9. 186-201. DOI: 10.1007-s40501-022-02266-2

Morris, P. A., Albanesi H. P., & Cassidy, S. (2019). Student veterans' perception of barriers and environment at a high-density veteran enrollment campus. *Journal of Veterans Studies*, *4*(2),180-202. https://journal-veterans-studies.org/articles/10.21061/jvs.v4i2.102

Nichter, B., Tsai, J., & Pietrzak, R. H. (2023). Prevalence, correlates, and mental health burden associated with homelessness in U.S. military veterans. *Psychological Medicine*, 53, 3952-3962.
https://doi.org/10.1017/S0033291722000617

Osborne, N. J. (2016). From camouflage to classroom: Designing a transition curriculum for new student veterans. *Journal of Postsecondary Education and Disability*, *29*(3), 285–292.
https://files.eric.ed.gov/fulltext/EJ1123804.pdf

Perkins, D. F., Davenport, K. E., Morgan, N. R., Aronson, K. R., Bleser, J. A., McCarthy, K. J., Vogt, D., Finley, E. P., Copeland, L. A., & Gilman, C. L. (2023). The influence of employment program components upon job attainment during a time of identity and career transition. *International Journal for Educational and Vocational Guidance*, 23, 695-717.
https://link.springer.com/article/10.1007/s10775-022-09527-1

Randles, R., & Finnegan, A. (2021). Veteran help-seeking behavior for mental health issues: A systemic review. *BMJ Military Health*, 168. pp 99-104.
Doi: 10.1136/bmjmilitary-2021-001903

Ravindran, C., Morley, S. W., Stephens, B. M., Stanley, I. H., & Reger, M. A. (2022). Association of suicide risk with transition to civilian life among US military service members. *JAMA Network Open*, *3*(9): e2016261.
doi: 10.1001/jamanetworkopen.2020.16261

Riggs, K. R., Hoge, A. E., DeRussy, A. J., Montgomery, A. E., Holmes, S. K., Austic, E. L., Pollio, D. E., Kim, Y., Varley, A. L., Gelberg, L., Gabrielian, S. E., Blosnich, J. R., Merlin, J., Gundlapalli, A. V., Jones, A. L., Gordon, A. J., Kertesz, S. G. (2020). Prevalence of and risk factors associated with nonfatal overdose among veterans who have experienced homelessness. *JAMA Network Open*, *3*(3):e201190.
doi: 10.1001/jamanetworkopen.2020.1190

Rose, S., VanDenKerkhof, E., & Schaub, M. (2018). Determinants of successful transition literature review. *Journal of Military, Veteran and Family Health*, *4*(1). Doi: 10.3138/jmvfh.4313

Saulnier, K. G., Bagge, C. L., Ganoczy, D., Bahraini, N. H., Jagusch, J., Hosanagar, A., Ilgen, M. A., & Pfeiffer, P. N. (2025). Suicide risk evaluations and suicide in the veterans health administration. *JAMA Network Open*, *8*(2):e2461559.
doi: 10.1001/jamanetworkopen.2024.61559

Sherman, M. D. (2018). The support and family education (SAFE) program: Mental health facts for families. *Psychiatric Services*, *54*(1), 35-37.
https://psychservices.psychiatryonline.org.

Shields, J., Pechek, A. A., Brinck, E. A., & Sprong, M. E. (2020). Strategies for improving employment outcomes of veterans diagnosed with post-traumatic stress disorder (PTSD). *The Rehabilitation Professional*, *28*(4), 225-244.
https://www.researchgate.net/publication/361948192_Strategies_for_Improving_Employment_Outcomes_of_Veterans_Diagnosed_with_Post-Traumatic_Stress_Disorder_PTSD/link/62ce26875dc7555897cd9051/download?_tp=eyJjb250ZXh0Ijp7ImZpcnN0UGFnZSI6InB1YmxpY2F0aW9uIiwicGFnZSI6InB1YmxpY2F0aW9uIn19

Shue, S., Matthias, M. S., Watson, D. P., Miller, K. K., & Munk, N. (2021). The career transition experiences of military Veterans: A qualitative study. *Military Psychology*, *33*(6), 359–371.
https://doi.org/10.1080/08995605.2021.1962175

Stahley, A. A., Daley, K. M., & McLain, R. (2022). Stories from the academic front: Leveraging veterans' voices. *Journal of Health and Human Experience*, *VI*(2), 66-79.
https://jhhe.sempervifoundation.org/pdfs/v6n2/04%20Stahley.pdf

Timko, C., Nash, A., Owens, M. D., Taylor, E., & Finlay, A. K. (2020). Systemic review of criminal and legal involvement after substance use and mental health treatment among veterans: Building towards needed research. *Substance Abuse: Research and Treatment*, 14. 1-13. DOI: 10.1177/1178221819901281

Tsai, J., Havlik, J., Howell, B. A., Johnson, E., & Rosenthal, D. (2022). Primary care for veterans experiencing homelessness: A narrative review of the homeless patient aligned care team (HPACT) model. *J Gen Intern Med*, *38*(3), 765-783.
DOI: 10.1007/s11606-022-07970-y

Umucu, E. (2023). Employment and rehabilitation for veterans with chronic conditions and disabilities: Strengths, challenges, opportunities, and policy suggestions. *Rehabilitation Counselors and Educators Journal*, *12*(1). https://doi.org/10.52017/001c.55516

U.S. Department of Veterans Affairs. (2025). *Federal Benefits for Veterans, Dependents, Survivors, and Caregivers, 2025 Edition, Pamphlet* 80-25-1. https://www.benefits.va.gov/benefits/media-publications.asp#benefitSummaries

Vaudreuil, R., Langston, D. G., Magee, W. L., Betts, D., Kass, S., & Levy, C. (2022). Implementing music therapy through telehealth: Considerations for military populations. *Disability and Rehabilitation, 17*(2), pp. 201-210. DOI: 10.1080/17483107.2020.177.5312

Whitworth, J., Smet, B., & Anderson, B. (2020). Reconceptualizing the US Military's Transition Assistance Program: The Success in Transition Model. *Journal of Veterans Studies, 6*(1), 25-35.
DOI: https://doi.org/10.21061/jvs.v6i1.144

Young, S. L., & Phillips, G. A. (2019). Veterans' adjustment to college: A qualitative analysis of large-scale survey data. *College Student Affairs Journal, 37*(1), 39-53. DOI: 10.1353/csj.2019.0003

Ziencik, C. (2020). Transition from the military to higher education: A case study of the transition assistance program. *Journal of Veterans Studies, 6*(22), 30-45. DOI: https://doi.org/10.21061/jvs.v6i2.178

www.ingramcontent.com/pod-product-compliance
Lightning Source LLC
Chambersburg PA
CBHW050632160426
43194CB00010B/1644